MOZART
AND HIS
OPERAS

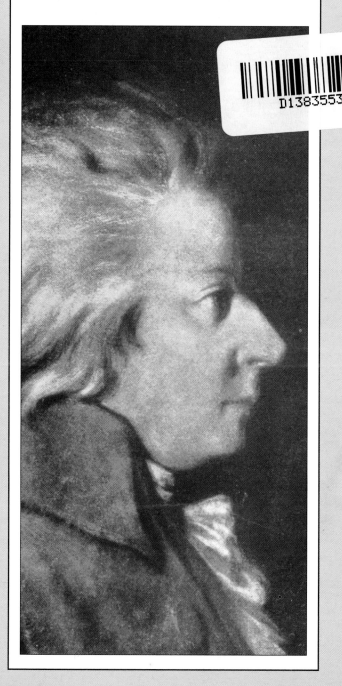

Mozart at thirty, in the year of *The Impresario*, *The Marriage of Figaro* and three of his greatest piano concertos.

Mozart

by Martin Hoyle

The World *of* Opera

● OMNIBUS PRESS

British Library Cataloguing in
Publication Data:
A catalogue record for this book is
available from the British Library.

Copyright © Martin Hoyle 1996
Order No.OP47814
ISBN 0-7119-5498-4

First published in softback in the UK
in 1996 by Omnibus Press
(a division of Book Sales Limited),
8/9 Frith Street, London W1V 5TZ.

Exclusive Distributors:
Book Sales Limited,
8/9 Frith Street, London W1V 5TZ.
Music Sales Corporation,
257 Park Avenue South, New York,
NY10010, USA.
Music Sales Pty Limited,
120 Rothschild Avenue, Rosebery,
NSW2018, Australia.

To the Music Trade only:
Music Sales Limited,
8/9 Frith Street, London W1V 5TZ.

Cover designed by Michael Bell Design.
Text edited and designed by
Three's Company, 5 Dryden Street,
London WC2.
Cover photograph courtesy of Pictorial Press.

Printed and bound in Great Britain by
Butler & Tanner Ltd, Frome and London

Contents

Picture acknowledgments
Picture research by Image Select:
Elizabeth Davis
Alexander Goldberg

Picture credits
Catherine Ashmore/Zoë Dominic
Photographs: pp. 99, 111
Clive Barda: pp. 91, 143
Zoë Dominic Photographs: p. 135
Hulton Deutsch: p. 69
Image Select: pp. 1, 7, 8, 15, 17, 19,
21, 23, 25, 29, 31, 32, 45, 46, 47,
51, 53, 58, 61, 63, 71, 75, 81, 83,
85, 95, 101, 102, 105, 107, 113,
118, 127, 133, 139, 144-145, 146,
153
Popperfoto: pp. 12, 39, 66-67, 150-
151
Ann Ronan at Image Select: pp. 65,
125

Foreword

One of my favourite stories about Mozart concerns those round, expensively-wrapped and rather luxurious chocolates that abound in German-speaking countries, along with the other Mozartian paraphernalia that makes its vendors a fortune denied to the little man who was its inspiration. They bear the face of Mozart; they are named after him. They are inescapable in Vienna and Salzburg.

The grandmother of a friend of mine would scold her grandchildren when they clamoured for these treats. She would hold one up for them to examine. 'You see that man in the powdered wig? That's Mozart. These sweets are expensive, rich and delicious. They cost a lot of money; he never had such money. Just remember that as you eat it.'

Today we listen to Mozart's music at the turn of a switch, we jet to international festivals or queue for standing-room at our local *Volksoper*. We take for granted access to such marvels and, however much we grumble, most of us can afford at least a CD of these luxury goods – luxuries such as *Così fan tutte*, a fondant with a bitter aftertaste, or the crunchy cracknel of *Figaro*, or the dark luscious liqueur of *Don Giovanni*. We feel the richer for these wonders that failed to enrich their creator.

In the context of his hard-working and sometimes hard-playing life, with its frustrations, disappointments and even hum-drum moments, these almost perfect artifacts seem all the more miraculous. Just remember Mozart the next time you're moved or exhilarated by his operas. Better still, obey the injunction, proudly written out in English, dedicating a few bars of music to an English acquaintance, a request almost unbearably touching: 'Don't never forget your true and faithfull friend, Wolfgang Amadé Mozart.'

Martin Hoyle
London 1996

Chapter 1

Early years: *Influences and Experiments*

It was Rossini who, speaking of Mozart, said something to the effect that 'in my youth he was my master, in my manhood my guide and in my old age he will be my consolation.'

This is understandable enough to a post–*Amadeus* age. Mozart has always been accessible. He wrote tunes. His style conforms to the image we have of the *ancien régime*: graceful, elegant, stylish, aristocratic – though his music is

Leopold Mozart: successful provincial civil servant, author of a standard work on violin-playing, manager of a successful family troupe and possessive father.

Mozart was born on 27 January 1756 on the third floor of what is now 9 Getreidegasse in rooms rented from a grocer.

robust enough to survive such treatments as 'Mozart 40' and the once heard never-forgotten rock version of the *Rondo alla Turca* with its refrain of 'Satin shoes, satin shoes, keep my Cinderella dancing'. He even seems to have become the posthumous author of a piece called 'Elvira Madigan', though purists may seek the title in vain among his piano concertos.

Mozart is so popular he's taken for granted. This was illustrated by a recent radio game where the panellists had to argue which great composer to keep in a balloon that was losing height and which to jettison. At the end it was discovered that nobody had mentioned Mozart at all. 'But we assumed he was there,' they protested. Everyone does.

Yet has any great composer been subjected to so many misunderstandings both in his lifetime and after it? His operas, above all, have suffered from their very ability to change complexion according to the colours of the time – any time – and sometimes clash with them. The Austrian authorities were uneasy about Don Giovanni's inflammatory cry of '*viva la libertà!*' and the censors moved in. But it didn't stop there. *Così fan tutte* virtually disappeared for the whole of the nineteenth century: the Romantics were dismayed by its apparent cynicism while moralists were shocked by the seeming flippancy with which it treated sexual relationships. *The Magic Flute* has been both derided as fairy-tale doggerel and overloaded with symbolic solemnity. Mozart was indeed for all times. It's right and proper that his operas haven't been venerated museum pieces in a glass case; but the obverse side of the coin is that they've come in for their fair share of distortion, misrepresentation and simple incomprehension. They still come up smiling. As W.H. Auden put it in the prologue to his translation of *The Magic Flute*, 'a work that lives two hundred years is tough/And operas, God knows, must stand enough.'

Mozart started his career as an infant prodigy on keyboards and violin who composed from the age of six. He was trotted around the courts of Europe and dandled on royal knees. At fourteen he was commissioned to compose an opera for the ducal theatre in Milan – but then he had had three operas to his credit by the age of twelve. By the time he died at thirty-five he was sick with money worries, deep in debt, and worn out by professional disappointments (though the accepted story that he was buried in a pauper's grave is an exaggeration; his modest funeral and unmarked burial place were in accordance with the practice of many in the enlightened middle classes and encouraged by the government in the cause of economy). The irony is that Mozart was not, like so many prodigies, a dazzling comet, a meteor soon burnt out. His works ripened into genius as he matured. Nowhere is this more obvious than in his operas. The extraordinary leap between *Die Entführung aus dem Serail* and *Le nozze di Figaro* a mere six years later – in terms of command of the stage and expressing complex psychology in music – would have taken another man half a lifetime.

The Prince-Archbishop of Salzburg; a benign and indulgent employer of the Mozarts, unlike his successor.

In 1756 the Duc de Richelieu invented mayonnaise (he also enjoyed giving nude dinner parties; perhaps it's best not to conjecture whether the two are connected). There broke out the Seven Years' War, which marked the last battle in which a king of England led his troops in person. There were tensions on the American continent between British and French interests. And on a snowy January day in the Austrian city of Salzburg, Johann Chrysostom Wolfgang Theophilus Mozart was born.

Leopold Mozart

His family background was certainly conducive to any musical talent a child might show. His father Leopold was author of a respected book, a *Treatise on the Fundamental Art of Violin Playing*, published the year of Wolfgang's birth, which would remain a standard work among teachers of the instrument for many years after his – and his son's – death. Leopold came from a middle-class professional background; his family were bookbinders in Augsburg and he had been in the service of the Prince-Archbishop of Salzburg for thirteen years. He had worked his way up from fourth violin in the court orchestra to court composer and finally vice-Kapellmeister. The Kapellmeister was the director of music, and music was a feature of every civilised mid-European princely court, complete with tame composer hired to write music for special occasions, religious services or simply background listening. Leopold remained, sometimes rather nervously, based at Salzburg, even when his wayward and gifted son quarrelled with one of the more arrogant prince-bishops and shook the dust of the city from his feet.

Leopold's wife, Anna Maria, was the daughter of a civil servant, who was respectable but dogged by ill health and debt-ridden. Of the Mozarts' seven children Wolfgang was the youngest. He and his elder sister were the only two to survive: a common enough ratio in those days. Maria Anna, nicknamed Nannerl, was four years older than her brother, who was fascinated when she began harpsichord lessons at the age of eight. The little boy's first love was mathematics: he covered walls, floor and furniture with chalk figures, with an engrossed single-mindedness that he would later show towards music. The court musician, Johann Andreas Schachtner, was to recall how the child Mozart, playing his own small violin, declared from memory that Schachtner's own instrument was tuned half a quarter-tone lower. The grown-up fetched his fiddle and compared it with the child's:

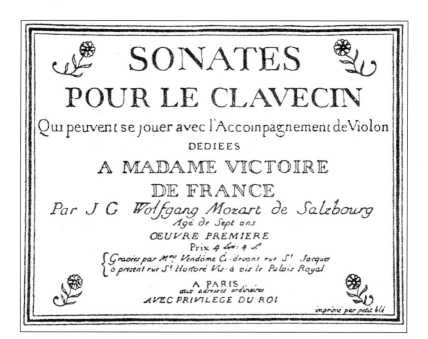

Mozart was only seven when his first work appeared in print: two pairs of keyboard sonatas.

the boy was right. Besides being accurate, little Wolfgang's musical ear was sensitive to an extreme. He particularly disliked any impurity of tone in wind instruments. When Schachtner blew his trumpet, the boy reacted as if it had been a loaded pistol and nearly fainted in distress.

Wolfgang composed his first piece at five and began his travels – as a 'prodigy of nature' at the harpsichord – at the age of six. In today's terms, father Leopold seems to have caught on to the practice of PR and publicity fairly quickly. For all his affection and pride towards his offspring, he was prone to complain bitterly if financial rewards were disappointing, and soon learnt the value of advance advertising ('the greatest wonder in all Germany') in the press along the route.

It would be a mistake, however, to think of Leopold as a pushy and ruthless 'show-biz' father. The little family was close and affectionate; and young Wolfgang was full of energy and enthusiasm. His sister later recalled his high spirits and readiness for pranks. An English observer in London recorded how the prodigy left the keyboard in the middle of a display of virtuosity to play with a favourite cat. It was in father Leopold's interest, after all, to keep his children happy and in good health: the mere hint of illness in small-pox conscious Vienna, for instance, and the audience stayed away.

At the Viennese court
The highlight of Mozart's early career as peripatetic prodigy

The six-year-old Mozart plays before the Austrian Empress Maria Theresa.

was, of course, a stay in Vienna. Austria was the centre of the Holy Roman Empire and Vienna was its heart, from where the Habsburg monarchy held sway over the Archduchy of Austria and kingdoms of Bohemia and Hungary, not to mention possessions in northern Italy, including the Grand Duchy of Tuscany. Vienna itself was the centre of an astonishing polyglot culture drawn from the Austro-Hungarian empire: Bohemians, Slovenians, Serbs, Croatians, Italians and Magyars were among the races that looked to the Austrian capital as their political and cultural centre, though Prague and Budapest both counted as royal capitals within the empire, and both – as Mozart came to appreciate in the case of Prague – had their own artistic identities. The Austrian court had a distinguished history of musical culture going back to the mid-seventeenth century, when Ferdinand III had sent his musicians to study in Italy with the result that Italian opera had established itself in Vienna shortly after. The father of the Empress Maria Theresa, Charles VI, had kept a permanent strength of 140 musicians and had his daughters' voices trained (though the future empress herself was less interested in music).

The Emperor Francis called the young performer from Salzburg a 'little wizard'. The little wizard showed how undaunted he was by the imperial pomp of Vienna by jumping on to the empress' lap and flinging his arms round her. To the little princess who helped him up when he slipped on the highly polished floor he declared he would like to marry her; but Maria Antonia's destiny lay in France as Marie Antoinette.

Leopold Mozart with his children Wolfgang and Maria Anna ('Nannerl').

It was, as Dickens would observe from a later viewpoint, the best of times and the worst of times. The old feudalism was breaking down, the certainties of organised religion were being called into question, rationalism had characterised the eighteenth century and the study of natural sciences was undermining old beliefs and superstitions. They would be attacked from another quarter too: in Germany the *Sturm und Drang* ('storm and stress') movement would herald the Romantics with their emphasis on passionate feelings, not merely the relatively controlled emotional mode of sensibility, and the individual.

The little archduchess that the infant Mozart wanted to marry would end her life on the guillotine. Another sort of revolution, that would make the off-shore island of Britain into the foundry and workshop of the world, was already under way. But in some areas the old paternalism went unchallenged. In central Europe musicians, for instance, were dependent on patrons ; there were well-paid individual commissions, certainly, but it was better to hold a permanent court position (in liberal Britain a growing middle class had enabled more to lead a free-lance existence). Leopold Mozart, an educated man of some social standing when his son was born, was in government employ, and embodies the moderately successful civil servant, received in respectable society, if not on a par with the nobility. His son would have more trouble in defining himself socially.

Mozart's Grand Tour

Vienna was almost a trial run for the Mozart family's Grand Tour of 1763. The seven-year-old Wolfgang was accompanied by his violinist/pianist sister and, of course, proud father Leopold. Various cities in the Holy Roman Empire – notably Mannheim, where they heard an orchestra that was amongst the greatest in Europe – marked the little family's passage to Paris, where they stayed for five months, with visits to Versailles. Mozart never seems to have warmed to the Parisian public, even when he revisited France as a young man. The elements of fashion and snobbery, formality and shallowness, later repelled him. As a child he was cross that the king's mistress, Madame de Pompadour, refused to kiss him as the Empress of Austria had done.

The splendour and formality of the French court contrasted with relatively relaxed England, where the Mozarts arrived in April 1764, and where the prodigy composed his first symphony at the age of eight. The fifteen months in England

Farinelli (real name Carlo Broschi) was the greatest of the castrati who dominated Italian opera in the generations immediately preceding Mozart's maturity. As an elderly celebrity he met the teenage Mozart in Italy.

proved successful, apart from the elder Mozarts' reservations about English beer, weather and fashions. They went to the races, visited Canterbury, and in short behaved like tourists, when not amazing the English musical public.

Johann Christian Bach ('the London Bach') became an influential friend and introduced the boy to a more immediate melodic style than the German school the Mozarts were used to (though Mozart himself didn't discover the music of the great Johann Sebastian, his friend's father, until adult maturity, when he was bowled over). The boy was already showing a hankering to compose opera, possibly inspired by meeting two celebrated castrati, Tenducci and Manzuoli; but the ambition would not be realised until he was all of eleven. Meanwhile he continued to take in the varied influences which he would observe at work even in the one form of opera.

Italian opera

The eighteenth century was dominated by Italian opera. German composers such as the London-based Handel and

Christoph Willibald
Gluck: a great reformer
of the operatic form,
and as influential in
Paris as in Vienna.

later Haydn had used current Italian forms; even the sonata form in instrumental music is a descendant of the operatic aria with its alternating quick-slow-quick sections. Italian musicians sought, and frequently found, their fortunes all over Europe in a process of musical colonisation that made Italian the lingua franca for anyone concerned with music.

The first half of the century had seen the rise of *opera seria*, usually based on a theme from mythology or classical history and treated as a succession of solo arias, frequently a dazzling showcase for singers. It was the preferred vehicle for gala and state occasions, when distinguished spectators could be flattered by allegorical allusions and elevated by high-flown sentiments. The *primo uomo* was usually a castrato; a *prima donna* soprano and leading tenor completed the line-up of principals, supported by minor characters, usually also led by a castrato.

To modern sensibilities the castrato phenomenon seems not only inhuman but puzzling, especially when we hear of such heroic characters as Hercules being portrayed by these unmanned singers, all presumably male sopranos or altos. Yet according to contemporary accounts the castrato voices had astonishing strength – perhaps the best comparison is with a trumpet – and were sufficiently virile to inspire female fans to swoon, sob and tear their clothes off much as their successors do for Tom Jones. It is also intriguing to find that some castratos married and even had children – for medical reasons mercifully well outside the scope of this book!

The libretto form for *opera seria* was honed, polished and perfected by the long-lived librettist Pietro Metastasio, born in 1698 and still alive in his eighties, when Mozart was already established in opera. Although he was from a different cultural and musical epoch, nevertheless his pen would, ironically, provide Mozart with one of his last operatic subjects in *La Clemenza di Tito*. It was Metastasio who took the French classical drama as epitomised by the works of Corneille and Racine as his model: no unseemly comic elements, no distracting extravagance of sentiment or action; instead an emphasis on compactness (if possible observing the

Mozart at the age of six, in the court dress given to him by the Empress Maria Theresa.

unities of time and place), clarity and dignity. This imposed a corset of restraint on the emotions depicted, and limited the psychological development of the characters.

Bad *opera seria* can stand for everything stilted and artificial, and by Mozart's time the form was already out-dated; but *Tito* would breathe life into these marble statues with their buttoned-up expressions of anguished nobility. One definition of a masterpiece is not that it breaks new ground but that it sums up and crystallises a form so perfectly that nobody can use it again. By those standards, *Tito* is both a masterpiece and the final salute to a dead form. It was ironic that Metastasio's innovations should themselves congeal into artificiality.

In due course another great operatic reformer appeared, a composer rather than a writer. Christoph Willibald Gluck also cleared away excrescences in the cause of music of austere grandeur and emotional directness. His revered position at the Austrian court, or more accurately his disproportionate salary, was a source of irritation and bewilderment to the young Mozart.

By Mozart's youth the classical form had become more flexible. Composers such as Galuppi and Jommelli worked in Germany and Austria making arias longer, more complicated and more emotionally expressive. The orchestra's role became more varied and more important. Ensembles began to feature as well as solo arias. Composers whose work Mozart would have known well, in some cases writing extra arias for interpolation into their operas, included Cimarosa, Paisiello (composer of the first *Barber of Seville*, the first opera drawn from a Beaumarchais play, even before Mozart's *Figaro*), Anfossi and Piccinni, whose *Buona Figliuola*, based on Samuel Richardson's novel of virtue besieged, *Pamela*, was an international smash hit and founded the form of *opera semiseria*.

Opera and *Commedia dell'arte*

By now we can perceive the emerging glories of Italian comic opera with mixed serious and comic elements, musical mood-changes and important chorus role. *Opera buffa* was earthy, usually involving complex amorous intrigue, cross-purposes, disguises and sprightly servants drawn from the *commedia dell'arte* tradition (and before that, the Roman Plautus). There was still an underlying morality, however. The vain, the mean, the affected, the cowardly – all were held up to ridicule. Other *commedia dell'arte* characters included the old

Maria Anna Thekla Mozart, nicknamed 'Bäsle' (little cousin), shared her cousin Wolfgang's sense of mischief and sometimes rude humour.

buffoon, usually a miser, often amorous and ripe for duping, the braggadocio military swashbuckler, the bogus scholar with his often nonsensical dog-Latin mumbo-jumbo (hence Despina's disguises in *Così fan tutte*). Young love triumphed and recognisable human emotions were expressed with sparkle and vivacity.

By the time Mozart had reached his maturity a serious element, usually manifested in the roles of the lovers, had transformed some characters into figures of refinement and nobility, while making the comic parts even earthier and coarser: the extremes of Donna Anna and Leporello in *Don Giovanni* had their antecedents on the contemporary stage, though Mozart alone could combine drama and comedy seamlessly and add extra dimensions to his ostensibly type-cast dramatis personae.

Apart from the Italian predominance in musical theatre there was German *Singspiel*. This was a mixture of speech and song, much influenced by English ballad opera, and not taken too seriously as an art form or in the salons of the native German princelings until the Emperor Joseph II founded a German National school to encourage native composers. The form had its origins in knockabout comedy with songs of Hanswurst, or Jack Sausage, the typical clown beloved of German tradition. The mixture of speech and music inspired some established composers such as Gluck, with his Islamic comedy *Die Pilgrime von Mekka*, and Dittersdorf, with his resoundingly successful *Der Apotheker und der Doktor*, but above all Mozart's *Entführung aus dem Serail* remains its greatest achievement. It also forms the basis for Mozart's last, exasperatingly mixed masterpiece of the comic and sublime, allegory and farce, about the birdman, the questing prince and the magic flute.

First dramatic work

Mozart's first dramatic work was *Apollo et Hyacinthus*, a 'Latin intermezzo', to be performed in the interval of a play during ceremonies at the Benedictine University at Salzburg, staged in costume with full scenic effects on May 13 1767. Students and boy choristers made up the cast, and beneath the conventional forms a warmth of feeling and a hint of characterisation can already be felt.

The following year's trip to Vienna was disappointing and marked by the two Mozart children's contracting smallpox. Vienna has always been a city of plots, intrigues and rivalries, and now Leopold Mozart found his 12-year-old son had to contend with the cabals and jockey for power like any hardened hack. Although, with the encouragement of the new Emperor, Joseph II, Mozart pressed ahead with his operatic ambitions, intrigues kept the finished product off the stage for nearly a year. 'All I can tell you is that a whole hell of musicians has risen up to prevent this display of a child's ability,' wrote a furious Leopold Mozart. 'A conspiracy has been formed to produce it extremely badly and thus ruin it.' When *La finta semplice* (The Pretended Simpleton) was finally staged it was not in Vienna but back in Mozart's home town of Salzburg. On the other hand, the child was avidly taking in the current trend-setters in opera: Hasse's *Partenope*, Gluck's *Alceste* and Piccinni's *La buona figluiola*.

Bastien und Bastienne

Meanwhile, some consolation was found in the friendship of Dr Franz Anton Mesmer, a fashionable medic whose 'cures by

magnetism' gave us the word mesmerism (and which were to be a subject of some humour in the adult Mozart's *Così fan tutte*). He commissioned a short comic work from the boy composer to be performed in the private theatre of his smart suburban home. *Bastien und Bastienne* is a gentle satire on Jean-Jacques Rousseau's *Le devin du village*, with its emphasis on primitive innocence and pastoral simplicity. Mozart's setting, unveiled in October 1768, is amazingly assured and invests the work with a charm that rather defeats the purpose of the intended parody. The slender plot concerns Bastienne (soprano) who believes that her Bastien (tenor) no longer loves her. The wise man of the village Colas (baritone) advises her to be cool towards her lover and at the same time informs Bastien that his sweetheart has lost interest in him. This naturally spurs the swain to redoubled ardour and the couple are reunited. The piece is sometimes performed by children.

Summoned back to Salzburg by the elder Mozart's employer, the Prince-Bishop, the family was rewarded with a production of *La finta semplice* in spring 1769. Based on a comedy by Goldoni, the typically *commedia*-like plot shows how the baroness Rosina, disguised as a simpleton, infatuates two brothers, silly Polidoro and the miserly Cassandro, both of whom she quite fancies, while her own brother manages to marry their sister. The work suffers from a lack of sympathetic characters, and the rollicking finales sound like Italian comic opera on auto-pilot, but there are touches, especially in the delicate use of woodwind, that hint at great things to come. Even so it was not heard in Britain until 1956 (from a touring provincial Austrian company) and the USA till 1961.

Mozart's mother and sister – at eighteen an accomplished teacher – remained behind when the 13-year-old and his father decided to try their fortunes in Italy. The indulgent Archbishop had made the boy 'Konzertmeister' (leader) of the Court Chapel, a great honour, and evidently intended to remind him of his duties to Salzburg, whatever success he might achieve in the south.

Like many northern Europeans, Mozart found Italy a revelation. It was at this time that he translated one of his Christian names Theophilus (or 'Gottlieb', to use the German form) into the Italian 'Amadeo' or 'Amadé'. And it was in Italy that Mozart struck up a deep friendship with the young English composer Thomas Linley (brother-in-law of the playwright Sheridan), Mozart's exact contemporary, who was to die by drowning at twenty-two. More important, Amadé was commissioned to write an opera.

Mitridate, re di Ponto

Mitridate, re di Ponto (Mithridates, King of Pontus) was premièred at the Teatro Regio Ducal, Milan, on December 26 1770. It has taken some time to find a wider public, though a recent handsome and stylised production at the Royal Opera in London has won praise. Again, there are signs of deepening emotional awareness in this complex story, based on Racine's *Mithridate,* of family strife and tangled loves. Farnace and Sifare, the sons of King Mithridates, both love Aspasia, though Farnace is betrothed to Ismene besides being allied to his father's enemies. However, honour and filial duty are redeemed when he avenges his father's defeat, and the dying king gives him his blessing.

Mozart revelled in the chance of writing for a larger orchestra than he had been used to (and possibly better, too,

Giambattista Martini –
Padre Martini – the
famous musical scholar,
who was impressed by
the teenage Mozart's
abilities on the boy's
first visit to Italy.

to judge by the horn obbligato he inserts into one aria), and
composing for star voices – though the latter caused the occasional bother: the tenor in the title-role was as fussy as the
breed is traditionally supposed to be and Mozart had to
rewrite his aria three times. Nevertheless, the work was a
huge success.

The same theatre saw the première of Mozart's next stage
piece, the 'dramatic serenata' *Ascanio in Alba* (October 17
1771), for the wedding celebrations of the Archduke
Ferdinand and Maria Beatrice d'Este. The libretto by the distinguished poet Parini recalls the stately allegorical masques
that used to grace the Stuart courts in England, with high-
flown language pointing a noble moral, garnished with flattering symbolic references to the eminent personages present.
The composer Johann Hasse remarked of his young rival –
with a generosity not common among practising artists of
whatever discipline – that 'this boy will eclipse us all.' His

generosity is all the more remarkable since his own new offering, *Ruggiero*, had proved an unexpected failure the night before.

Cynics may suspect that the sumptuous visual side of the production eclipsed the music; but the young archduke was sufficiently impressed to ask his mother the Empress if he could take Mozart on permanently. Maria Theresa replied with the famous letter in which she claims she couldn't understand how you could have any use for a composer 'or useless people of that sort', but she wouldn't stop him if it gave him pleasure! Her attitude sounds familiar to all who have studied the attitude to the arts of those who govern us . . .

Il sogno di Scipione

The following April saw an occasion of mixed excitement and sadness. The 'azione teatrale' *Il sogno di Scipione* (The Dream of Scipio) which Mozart had prepared for the jubilee of his kindly patron, the Prince Archbishop of Salzburg, instead was played to celebrate the installation of his successor. Archbishop Schrattenbach had died in December and Count Hieronymus Colloredo, though a reformer and a product of the enlightenment, was to prove, at least as far as Mozart was concerned, stingy and unsympathetic. *Scipione* recounts the legend of Scipio Aemilianus who, in a dream, is wooed by both Fortune and Constancy. Fortune represents her changeability as an attraction while Constancy plays the emotional blackmail card by showing him the ghosts of his father and grandfather. They urge him to save Rome. Scipio plumps for Constancy. The fifteen-year-old composer could do little with the already antiquated conventions of Pietro Metastasio's libretto (originally written in 1735), but the sense of occasion and pompous state is enhanced by chorus and trumpets.

The third Italian journey of the Mozarts, father and son, found them uneasy about their new patron (in private letters they referred to him by a code-name). It may be this that contributed to Amadé's depressions and – a rare thing for him – difficulty in working. The composition of his next opera for Milan was held up by the late arrival of some of the singers – the tenor who was to take the title-role turned up eight days before the première! Ironically, he was the least gifted of a cast that included the famous castrato Rauzzini (for whom Mozart wrote the *Exsultate, jubilate* with its famous 'Alleluia'), and Mozart felt so constricted by his limited talents that the role of Lucio Silla himself is the least interesting, musically and dramatically, in the opera.

Lucio Silla

Lucio Silla was first performed on December 26 1772 at the now familiar Teatro Regio Ducal. A mild success, it prompted no offer of further work from the Grand Duke, despite tentative feelers put out by Mozart. The plot, based loosely on Roman history, recounts how the dictator Lucius Sulla tried to force Giunia (Junia) to accept his hand, sending her fiancé Cecilio (Caecilius) into exile. Giunia denounces Lucio in public and is imprisoned, ready to die with her betrothed. Lucio is moved and pardons them.

Despite the practical difficulties he faced during the work's composition, Mozart's splendidly imposing overture, exciting use of the chorus and some dramatically stirring accompanied recitatives show the influence of the operatic reformers such as Gluck. There are experiments with the non-stop stretches of music, which further the development of the drama seamlessly, rather than breaking it up into isolated numbers. This looks forward to the great finales of the mature operas, not to mention a much later idea of continuous music drama, and a thrilling use of the orchestra. *Lucio Silla* is occasionally revived, though it reached Britain only in 1967 and the USA the year after.

At seventeen, Mozart was back in Salzburg and began to chafe at the provincialism of his home town, comparing it unfavourably with Vienna, which he found exciting, stimulating and friendly. Opera takes a back seat for the moment, but incidental music to a highly symbolic play by one Tobias Philipp von Gebler looks forward to *The Magic Flute* in many ways. In *Thamos, König in Ägypten* (Thamos, King of Egypt) good and evil battle it out with virtue triumphant (the definition of fiction, as Miss Prism points out in *The Importance of Being Earnest*; it is also the definition of much eighteenth-century *opera seria*, as opposed to the following century's romantic fondness for all-too-perishable goodness). The Egyptian setting, the moral polarisation and the pretext for solemn music (for chorus and orchestra including trombones) all anticipate Mozart's masonic comedy.

La finta giardiniera

Meanwhile Mozart continued his duties as court Kapellmeister with efficiency but not much enthusiasm, his real genius coming out in flashes as he developed the piano concerto and symphony. When the Elector of Bavaria offered the commission of a comic opera for the carnival season in Munich, Mozart leapt at the chance. He had enjoyed previ-

Mozart and Aloysia, his
first love among the
Weber sisters, though he
was to marry the
younger Constanze.

ous visits to the Bavarian capital and seems to have been in high spirits while composing *La finta giardiniera* (The Pretend Gardener, often known in England as *Sandrina's Secret*). Italian *opera buffa* was the model. As so often, rehearsals ran wildly behind schedule, the première was postponed, and the opera's reception (on January 13 1775), though both father and son reported a huge success to their correspondents, led to no further commissions.

The libretto by Giuseppe Petrosellini, already set by another composer, Pasquale Anfossi, is a typically convoluted comedy of disguise and cross-purposes. The Marchesa Violante has it put about that she is dead as a result of a violent quarrel with her lover Count Belfiore. In fact she disguises herself as a gardener, Sandrina, and works for the comically pompous mayor, Don Anchise (that rarity a *buffo* or comic tenor), whose daughter is now being wooed by Belfiore. The complications include comically conniving servants and no fewer than two bouts of madness. Another great Mozartian finale provides a solid block of continuous musico-theatrical architecture; and there is a glimpse of the smiling, tolerant irony that will suffuse and humanise the equally artificial (but with a far better libretto) *Così fan tutte*. A few years later Mozart revised the recitatives for a German translation in the *Singspiel* style with spoken dialogue. This version was played (and has been recorded) as *Die Gärtnerin aus Liebe*.

Il re pastore

Mozart left Munich disappointed by the lack of offers of more work. But irksome Salzburg held a consolation prize: another 'serenata' in honour of visiting Habsburg royalty. *Il re pastore* (The Shepherd King) is one more of those static, symbolic fables from classical myth loaded with allusions and compliments for its noble spectators. Mozart's setting of the libretto by Metastasio (another that had already been set years before in honour of a different Habsburg) tells of how the shepherd Aminta is placed on the throne of Sidon by Alexander the Great; how unhappy he is away from his beloved Elisa, especially when Alexander arranges his marriage to the daughter of the late tyrant – herself loved by his faithful counsellor. When the characters pluck up courage (rather like Servilia with the emperor Titus in Mozart's last opera, *La Clemenza di Tito*) to break it to Alexander how unhappy his good intentions are actually making them all, he lets the pastoral couple return to blissful rusticity and gives

the kingdom to his friend.

The stilted nature of the action and the circumscribed emotional range of this offering to the Archduke Maximilian Franz left Mozart little to do except provide sometimes ravishing music: Aminta's aria 'L'amerò, sarò costante', for instance, with its violin solo; and the delicate scoring for the orchestra that reminds us how the concerto had caught the young composer's interest: *Il re pastore* was first performed on April 23 1775, and between April and December Mozart produced no fewer than five violin concertos.

The Mannheim influence

Mozart's next operatic enterprise would be nearly four years ahead. In the meantime, the composer would experience adventure, hope and disillusion: his resignation from his Salzburg post, professional disappointments in Munich and Augsburg and, most importantly, the revelation provided by music in Mannheim. The Mannheim court orchestra, founded in the 1740s, had become one of the most famous in Europe and its influence shaped the development of the classical symphony. Among the many friends Mozart made in Mannheim was the tenor Anton Raaff who would play a great part (literally and metaphorically) in the composer's life in the near future. He also met the Elector Palatine Karl Theodore, who had just founded a German national theatre, and was excited by the nobleman's championship of native German culture. Yet despite the congenial life of Mannheim, Mozart had little in the way of profitable commissions though he felt entirely at home and composed easily. Money ran short and young Amadé received anxious letters from father Leopold, still in Salzburg.

In 1778 the composer made the momentous acquaintance of the Weber family, former landed gentry financially come down in the world. Fridolin von Weber was a music copyist; one of his five children, eighteen-year-old Aloysia, was a singer. Mozart fell in love with her, to the horrified disapproval of his father. Eventually the composer listened to reason and, after composing arias for his beloved, resumed the business of earning a living. He and his mother set off for Paris. In due time Mozart would marry one of Aloysia's sisters, Constanze, while another, Josefa, would launch the dazzling fury of the Queen of the Night in his last opera.

The stay in Paris was a disaster. Mozart found himself treated as a servant by the aristocracy of the *ancien régime* who, anyway, were as culturally chauvinistic as the French

Young Wolfgang writes to his father from Paris – a city he disliked for its snobbery and formality.

have been traditionally. As a crowning blow, among many professional disappointments and social humiliations, his mother died on July 3. Mozart lingered in Paris hoping for an opera commission and cheered by old friends from his childhood London visit, J.C. Bach and the castrato Tenducci. But he gave in to financial and emotional pressures and returned to Salzburg, making a rather sneaky detour (to the fury of his father) to Mannheim. Now it was Aloysia Weber who thought the young composer an unsuitable match. She had become a hugely successful soprano and made it plain that Mozart no longer interested her emotionally. His parting gift was a magnificent showpiece aria, 'Popoli di Tessaglia'. In the following year Aloysia would marry the Viennese court actor Josef Lange.

Zaide

In January 1779, at just 23, Mozart appeared to admit defeat and took up his duties as organist to the hated Prince-Archbishop of Salzburg. Life was brightened by the arrival of a travelling theatre company, for whom Mozart made the *Singspiel* version of *Le finta giardiniera*. More excitingly, the ensemble provided a pretext for another opera, or rather a *Singspiel*: *Zaide* is set in sixteenth century Turkey. The sultan's favourite, Zaide, falls in love with Gomatz, a European captive, and the couple decide to escape with the help of the overseer. The sultan finds out and swears revenge. The imprisoned Zaide defies him, the overseer begs him to spare the captives, and a quartet blends the tyrant's anger with the overseer's pity and the lovers' defiance.

Mozart never finished the work – its fragments were first performed on stage in Frankfurt in 1866 – but it gives a fascinating preview of that later work that charted 'the abduction from the seraglio' (*Die Entführung aus dem Serail*), and contains at least one exquisite aria: 'Ruhe sanft', tenderly sung by the heroine over the sleeping captive whom she has fallen in love with. The touring company was followed by another, led by a certain Schikaneder, man of the theatre, writer, comic, singer . . . . He and Mozart were to collaborate, with extraordinary results, later on.

Meanwhile Amadé was bored and frustrated, though he was visiting the theatre, and discovering especially Shakespeare among the classics and, among contemporaries, Lessing and the adventurous Frenchman, Beaumarchais. The latter's *Barber of Seville* had taken the stage five years before, launching Figaro on the world.

The house of Court Councillor Serrarius in Mannheim, where Mozart received free lodging in return for giving the Councillor's daughter music lessons.

But the most exciting development in Amadé's career came not from Salzburg but Munich. Karl Theodore, whom Mozart had last met in Mannheim, was now Elector of Bavaria. In the winter of 1780 a commission for an *opera seria* to mark the carnival season took Mozart in a high state of excitement back to the city he now vastly preferred to his home town. *Idomeneo, re di Creta* was written by the Salzburg court chaplain, G.B. Varesco. Even the unsympathetic Prince-Bishop must have felt flattered at this double honour to Salzburg and allowed his organist leave in the Bavarian capital in November.

With hindsight it is all too easy to divide history, or art, into boxes – as if one day the baroque architects and sculptors said 'Let's all be rococo from now on', or Shakespeare decided that his early phase was over and he was now starting on the plays of his middle period. But *Idomeneo* is such a thrilling work, showing such feeling for characterisation, economy of means and superb control of the forces at

33

his disposal that it must rank as the first great opera of the Mozart canon. Until now we have watched the young provincial assimilating and discarding – Italian melody, German orchestration, neo-classical austerity, baroque flourishes. From now on the composer we see marshalling his forces is undoubtedly an operatic genius. Mozart has found his voice.

Chapter 2

Idomeneo

Mozart arrived in Munich on November 8 1780, having probably already started composing *Idomeneo, re di Creta* before he left Salzburg. The pleasure at seeing his friend the tenor Anton Raaff was tempered by strains in their professional relationship. At sixty-seven Raaff naturally had his own ideas as to the demands of the title-role; the wonder is that Mozart felt able to give him the elaborate bravura aria 'Fuor del mar'.

In a series of letters to his father (who arrived, with Nannerl, in time for the dress rehearsal on January 27 1781, Amadé's twenty-fifth birthday) the composer reveals his theatrical as well as his musical concerns – the fact that Raaff and del Prato, the castrato playing Idamante, were apparently bad actors seems to have irritated him as much as their vocal shortcomings. Worries about the vocal state of his cast were more than balanced by the joy he took in writing for the Mannheim orchestra – Karl Theodore, now the Elector of Bavaria, had brought the band with him to Munich – and it shows in Mozart's first use of clarinets in opera, the confidence in a great oboist at his command, the splendour of horns, trumpets and timpani.

From Salzburg Leopold in his turn showered his son with good advice and, more importantly, acted as a go-between with the librettist, Gianbattista Varesco. The latter, who was also court chaplain, prevailed upon to produce what finally amounted to four versions of the libretto, evidently felt both professionally insulted and personally harassed at the number of alterations he was called on to make, both as a result of the singers' requirements and of the young composer's sense of dramatic rightness. It is hardly surprising that he eventually lost his temper and demanded a higher fee. Mozart, meanwhile, was in his element. 'My head and my hands are so full

The Mozart family: Wolfgang and Nannerl are at the keyboard while their father Leopold holds his violin and their mother, who had died in Paris on one of her son's tours, looks down from the portrait.

of Act 3,' he wrote in early January, 'that it would be no wonder if I turned into a third act myself.'

The première

After two postponements the first performance of this latest 'sacrifice opera' (a popular genre that included Gluck's *Iphigénie en Tauride* and *Alceste*, showing the noble self-abnegation of humans when confronted by divine will) took place on January 29 1781. It was a success, though after the initial acclaim public reaction cooled. People were taken aback by the dramatic directness, the emotional vividness, of the characterisation. Used to thinking of the work as an early Mozart, composed to a conventionally old-fashioned *opera seria* libretto, we tend to forget that even by the standards of Gluck's operatic reforms – sweeping away the irrelevant and artificial in favour of a starker, more dignified style – *Idomeneo* was pretty jolting.

Perhaps people were not ready for it. It had only three performances and does not seem to have been professionally revived in Mozart's lifetime. A performance by noble dilettanti in Vienna some years later prompted the composer to add 'Non temer, amato bene' (Beloved, do not fear), with its violin obbligato, harking back to the lyric sweetness of *Il re pastore*, and to give the castrato role of Idamante to a tenor.

Characters:
Idomeneo, King of Crete *tenor*
Idamante, his son *tenor/soprano/mezzo-soprano*
  (*originally castrato*)
Ilia, a captive Trojan princess *soprano*
Elettra, a Greek princess *soprano*
Arbace, the king's counsellor *tenor*
Voice of Neptune *bass*
High Priest of Neptune *baritone*

The overture sets the mood for the opera: stateliness and surging emotions. Despite the heart beating beneath the neo-classical draperies, Idomeneo still observes the dignified formalities. Throughout the opera the orchestra will provide the flourishes, curlicues and swags of the baroque framework while the vocal writing remains relatively restrained. That Mozart 'put the statue in the pit and the pediment on the stage' was a once common grumble. It would be more appropriate to say that, in *Idomeneo* at least, the orchestra performs the function of those trumpet-blowing cherubs and tritons we see in the margin of baroque maps; it provides the swagger of those ornate cartouches that grace heroic portraits. The humans hold their pose while the background, radiantly pastoral, menacingly overcast or vindictively turbulent, reflects the true state of their feelings.

Act 1

The curtain rises on the palace of Idomeneo, King of Crete. Ilia is a captive, daughter of Priam King of Troy, the city recently destroyed by the Greeks. Friendless, her family wiped out, the young princess muses in accompanied recitative on the contradictory feelings that confuse her. Her captor, Idomeneo, one of the Greek alliance, is rumoured to have drowned on his way home, his fleet destroyed in a terrible storm at sea. Any feelings of vengeful satisfaction she may have are softened by the realisation that she loves the king's son, Idamante. The prince had rescued her from shipwreck – the angry spirit of Neptune and his unpredictable ocean dominates the plot. Ilia unhappily believes that Idamante loves Elettra, another foreign princess and fugitive from her own bloody family history in Argos.

In the opera's first aria, 'Padre, germani, addio!' (Father, brothers, farewell) Ilia's predicament is defined. She remembers her dead father and brothers and, while she reproaches herself for loving a Greek, admits she could never hate him. The radiant opening phrases soon give way to a thoughtful mood, but hope keeps breaking through. Musically her character comes through as tender and concerned, loving and anxious, while breathless, broken phrases emphasise her grief.

Idamante enters with the news that his father may yet be safe: Minerva (pro-Greek) has apparently rescued him from the anger of Neptune (pro-Trojan). He declares his love for Ilia, who finds it hard to forget the bitterness of the past. In an aria 'Non ho colpa' (I am guiltless) Idamante blames the gods for making him love her, and exclaims he would kill himself if she commanded it. A declamatory opening to a swirling orchestral accompaniment soon melts as he confesses he adores her. Anger takes over when he protests his innocence. (Mozart cleverly entrusted the musical agility that suggests high emotion to the orchestra rather than the dubious voice of del Prato, the original Idamante.)

A procession of Trojan prisoners is freed: former enemies join in a chorus praising peace (triple time has a humanising effect on the pomp of the occasion). Only Elettra is outraged by the insult to the allies implied in Idamante's soft treatment of the enemy. Arbace, the king's confidant, brings news that Idomeneo has after all been drowned.

As the rest hurry out, Elettra is left alone, furious at this new turn of events. In a vigorous accompanied recitative she reflects that Idamante, now king, can dispose of his heart and his empire as he sees fit. Despite her battle-axe image, such little touches as a falling musical phrase to the words 'oh duol!'(oh grief) ensure that we never lose sight of the unhappy human being beneath the fury. This is as well, since she launches into an aria, 'Tutte nel cor vi sento' (All the furies of hell I feel in my heart), that expresses her anger, her jealousy and the desire for revenge on Ilia. The orchestra adds a superb layer of armour to her naked rage as emphatic repeated notes hammer home her determination.

Without a break, musically or emotionally, we move with almost cinematic speed to the next scene, with its spectacular double-chorus effect. The two choruses ('near' and 'distant', according to the libretto) implore the gods for mercy in the storm. In a mime scene specified by the libretto (sometimes disregarded in production), Neptune himself calms the sea, threateningly eyes the shipwrecked Idomeneo (yes, still alive), and disappears. The king's first words are underlined by orchestral waves gently ebbing away.

In a recitative Idomeneo laments the rash bargain he has made with the sea-god: in return for his life he will sacrifice the first living person he sees. The ensuing aria, 'Vedrommi intorno' (I shall see around me), begins in the sort of introspective mood Mozart would perfect with Fiordiligi's guilty self-analysis in 'Per pietà' (For pity's sake) in *Così fan tutte*. As the full horror of his compulsory sacrifice of an innocent victim sinks in, Idomeneo's music accelerates to an agitated conclusion: 'Qual spavento, qual dolore!' (What terror, what grief!).

Inevitably the first person who hastens along the sea-shore to welcome the king is his son Idamante. The irony of the situation is heightened by the fact that after Idomeneo's long absence at the Trojan war neither recognises the other. The orchestra bursts out at their final recognition, intensifying each mood as it represents Idamante's happy astonishment, Idomeneo's horrified recoil and subsequent rejection of his son, and the young man's amazed shock as his father flees from him. The controlled emotion of the accompaniment to the grief-stricken prince's 'Ah qual gelido orror' (Ah, what freezing horror) anticipates how the orchestra will tighten the screw of suspense when Donna Anna, going through the events that led to her father's murder, identifies Don Giovanni as her assailant. It leads Idamante into an aria, 'Il padre adorato' (Adored father), which contrasts his initial joy with his present hurt bewilderment.

Following an intermezzo, a march depicts the returning Cretan troops. A chorus in honour of Neptune, with solos in a lighter, more delicate vein, gives thanks to the sea-god and his attendant nymphs. The act ends ironically as the womenfolk joyfully embrace the homecoming warriors, unaware of their king's terrible vow.

Act 2

Act 2 opens with Arbace advising Idomeneo to send his son away while they seek some way to appease Neptune. The king decides to send Idamante with Elettra to Argos, her native land. Arbace proceeds to assure the king of loyalty in a florid aria, stylised and *galant*, to which the orchestra makes a richly elaborate contribution; and rather unhelpfully adds that monarchs have problems.

A scene between Idomeneo and the captive princess Ilia reinforces the poignancy of the situation as she affirms her regard for him as a second father and Crete as her new home. Delicate writing for woodwind expresses the fragility of Ilia's happiness, the bittersweet quality of her contentment.

Musing on her mixture of serenity and sorrow, Idomeneo realises Ilia loves his son. The following aria, 'Fuor del mar' (From the sea), is a magnificent outburst of protest: at once a bravura showpiece for the veteran tenor Raaff, who created the role, and a breathless psychological depiction of emotional turmoil, complete with trumpets and drums, as Idomeneo declares that Neptune will claim three victims – the sacrificial Idamante and his broken-hearted father and lover.

Elettra takes the stage in an uncharacteristically good mood. She looks forward to winning over Idamante on their forthcoming journey together. The accompaniment to her recitative is warm, graceful, major-key, and exudes calm happiness. An introduction of gavotte-like grace leads to an aria, 'Idol mio' (Beloved idol), of rather touching confidence in the future: another of Mozart's reminders that Elettra is not simply a fury but a woman in love.

She is summoned aboard by the sound of a march (faintly anticipating *Figaro*, Act 3) and joins the chorus in maintaining a lyrically optimistic mood, 'Placido è il mar' (How calm the sea). It comes as a shock to realise that the following Terzetto 'Pria di partir' (Before parting) is the first concerted number of the opera – Mozart's great complex ensembles are yet to blossom. Idamante begs to kiss his father farewell and Elettra expresses gratitude more formally. The sudden note of urgency in Idomeneo's reply, Idamante's increasing sorrow and Elettra's puzzlement subtly change the sunny mood and prepare us for the next crisis: a storm breaks over the harbour. As the terrified populace begs the gods for mercy, thunder rolls, the ships are struck by lightning and catch fire, and a monster emerges from the sea. Goaded into a confession (recitative over brilliantly stormy orchestral colours), Idomeneo admits his guilt to Neptune and demands that the god accept him rather than an innocent victim as a sacrifice. The storm continues, the chorus flees; the act ends with sudden quiet.

Act 3

Act 3 opens with dramatic irony. Ilia, unaware of the latest disaster, reflects on the mixed sorrow and relief she feels at Idamante's absence. In a ravishing aria, 'Zeffiretti lusinghieri' (Alluring breezes), she urges zephyrs to fly to her beloved with assurances of her devotion; and she commands the tender flowers watered with her tears to tell him that there was never such true love. A melancholy middle section is flanked by spring-like melodic freshness over a lightly-scored accompaniment, fleetingly conjuring up the Elysian landscape of Gluck's *Orpheus*.

Idamante comes to tell her he must kill the monster or die in the attempt. Inevitably the young couple reveal their love, and Ilia's passionate recitative is gently nudged by the orchestra straight into their duet ('S'io non moro', If I do not die), another example of Mozart's flexibility in keeping mood and drama going without a break. The final section is in the triple time so often used to evoke the pastoral and idyllic.

Idomeneo and Elettra enter and quickly grasp the situation. In a tense exchange Idamante questions his father; Idomeneo is evasive but urges his son to flee; Ilia expresses her love; and Elettra seethes with anger.

The following quartet is surely the first great operatic ensemble of the Mozart canon. 'Andrò ramingo e solo,' (Alone, a wanderer I go) sings Idamante, resigned to wandering the earth in lonely exile; Ilia swears to stay with him till death; Idomeneo laments Neptune's cruelty; and Elettra broods on vengeance. Within an apparently rigid framework, four different characters express their emotions in a wonderfully rich and complex résumé of the action so far. The quartet may not in fact further the action but it crystallises the situation and the psychology of the main players. With one of those unexpected and heart-stopping strokes of musico-theatrical rightness, Mozart ends the ensemble quietly, with Idamante's lone voice affirming his intention to go into exile. He leaves.

Arbace brings news of a vast crowd outside the palace with the high priest of Neptune at their head. Idomeneo hurries off and Arbace reflects unhappily on a Crete devastated by divine wrath. The orchestral accompaniment uses strings with depth and warmth – the garrulous old counsellor is evidently a good man – and in the subsequent aria 'Se colà nei fati è scritto' (If thus it is written by fate) Arbace nobly offers himself for sacrifice. Omitted at the Munich première, the aria could be criticised in theatrical terms for holding up the action and lessening the tension, but paints a touching picture of the devoted old retainer.

In the palace square, subjected to the High Priest's divine authority, Idomeneo reveals the truth to his shocked people at last: the intended victim is his own son. He leaves in search of Idamante while the chorus sings in response to his declaration 'Oh voto tremendo!' (O terrible vow). The High Priest's solo is over triple time accompaniment, here not symbolic of graceful pastoralism but dragging footsteps, an inexorable, throbbing ache: compare the Count's cross-examination of Figaro in the Act 2 finale of the later opera – another of *Idomeneo's* foretastes of things to come.

To a march the king enters the great hall of Neptune's temple. In a cavatina of serenade-like delicacy the king, joined by the chorus, begs Neptune to abate his rage. This gingerly obsequious approach is interrupted by a triumphant chorus: Idamante has killed the monster. Idomeneo's fears that this will enrage Neptune all the more are dispelled by the sight of his son, clothed in white and draped in garlands. The prince has learned of his father's vow, realises the king's rejection of him was due to love, and is resolved to fulfil his father's promise. In one of the longest accompanied recitatives in Mozart opera the dialogue between the two shows the young man's determination to face this unnatural sacrifice. He urges his father to cherish Ilia as a daughter; and in assertive, almost combative, tones, he declares he has no fear of death but will go happily to the afterlife if his beloved can enjoy life and peace (aria, 'No, la morte io non pavento' – No, I do not fear death).

It is in fact Ilia herself who brings matters to a head: as Idomeneo raises the knife to slay his son, she rushes in and offers herself as a substitute victim, prompting Elettra's first comment for some time – the rather inadequate 'Oh qual contrasto', the equivalent of 'what a turn-up for the book!'.

The earth shakes; Neptune's statue moves; the High Priest falls into a trance before the altar. The petrified crowd is frozen into silence. A deep voice, Neptune himself, announces in curt phrases that love has triumphed and that Idamante and Ilia can reign in Idomeneo's place. The judgement is almost perfunctory in tone, but it is lent weight by the brass section. It illustrates Mozart's conviction that ponderous supernatural pronouncements should be kept brief and pithy. 'If the speech of the ghost in Hamlet were not so long,' he wrote to his father, 'it would be more effective.'

Elettra recovers herself sufficiently to let rip against the happy ending. The orchestral thrust angrily echoes her fury in the recitative leading to her spitfire aria 'D'Oreste, d'Aiace'. She departs after urging horned serpents to tear out her heart (her domestic staff is very different from Ilia's zephyrs): the most varied character in the opera, whose music ranges from the lovingly confident to the implacably jealous, she looks forward to the range of Donna Anna (*Don Giovanni*) or Vitellia (*Clemenza*).

In Idomeneo's long recitative of abdication the grateful relaxation of tension is almost palpable. In the long, lyrical aria 'Torna la pace' (Peace returns), he looks forward to a vigorous and serene old age. The metaphor of an old tree blooming again hints at the triumph of the natural over the unnatural – the decrees of the gods have been contrasted with benign nature throughout the opera – perhaps a disguised criticism of those reactionary forces that were seen to be repressing reason and humanity in the eighteenth century.

Dramatically it could be argued that the tension has dropped so much that Idomeneo's ostentatiously elaborate vocal line dissipates it totally; but that would be as nothing compared with the actual performance of the ballet music following the final chorus. Anyone who has seen it in performance knows that this extra quarter-hour tacked on to the opera is a case of gilding the lily and decidedly too much of a good thing, though individual excerpts give glimpses of future marvels: a melancholy minor-key passage pre-echoes one of the great piano concertos, and a gavotte which has become a favourite concert piece tinkled out by the most unlikely instrumental combinations. No, better to leave *Idomeneo* with its protagonist, noble, eloquent, with the pulse of life in his veins, defying the stilted libretto and contrived situations, thanks to Mozart's magically humanising touch.

Chapter 3

The Abduction from the Seraglio

However short-lived the triumph of *Idomeneo* was to prove, Mozart felt sufficiently confident to challenge his Salzburg employer's attitude: the attitude, that is, of a master towards his servant. The composer bitterly resented being relegated to downstairs, as it were, when he knew he belonged upstairs with the gentry – not for any reason of social snobbery but through his talent; and the young Mozart had no doubts about his talent.

The Prince-Archbishop's motives are puzzling; he was neither a philistine nor a reactionary in most things, but his treatment of Mozart shows a desire to slap down this cocky little member of his staff. The composer's protracted leave of absence in Munich (originally only granted until mid-December) must have looked like a deliberate snub to his

Mozart's residence in his unloving, and eventually unloved, home town of Salzburg.

45

Aloysia Weber, now married to the court actor Joseph Lange, and a famous singer in her own right.

employer; and the leisurely pace as he sauntered back to join the princely household, currently in Vienna, by mid-March, after a family visit to Augsburg, must have looked like insolence.

On the other hand, it seems outrageous that at meals Mozart should be seated below the valets and above the cooks. The infant prodigy who had sat on Maria Theresa's lap, kissed Marie Antoinette and charmed Queen Charlotte in London, whose music was requested by princes and electors – and who certainly didn't hesitate to stride up to nobility to chat at social occasions while other musicians hovered nervously in the background – was ranked as not much better than a footman. He was even refused permission to give concerts, which might have earned him a considerable amount.

By May there had been a showdown and the enraged Archbishop had dismissed an equally furious Mozart. 'I am still seething with rage,' he wrote to his father. 'He called me a lout and a dissolute wretch and told me to be off . . . . Now please be cheerful for my happiness is just beginning.' Nevertheless, a go-between, the sensible Count Arco, seems to have kept the Archbishop ready to take Mozart back, constantly urging the composer to swallow his pride and warning him of the difficulties of freelance life in fickle Vienna. By June it was apparent that Mozart, boasting of being as proud as a peacock, would never give in and he was finally – literally – kicked out.

The composer was soon lodging with his old friends the Webers. Aloysia, married to the actor Josef Lange, was out of reach, but Amadé was drawn to her sister Constanze. Professionally, too, life took a hopeful turn when a commission arrived from the writer Gottlieb Stephanie for an opera, a *German* opera, for the Vienna Burgtheater. By the 1780s German opera had at least a potential champion in the shape of the Austrian Emperor Joseph II. A reformer by nature who took his duty as ruler of a multitude of heterogeneous central European races extremely seriously, he saw culture, particularly the theatre, as a potentially unifying factor in the Austro-Hungarian Empire. Anxious to see a national school of music theatre emerge, he had established the Burgtheater as a state institution.

Not that creativity or backstage politics always run smoothly. Stephanie's book for his 'comic *singspiel*' in three acts, an arrangement of *Bellmont und Constanze* by the Leipzig businessman Christoph Friedrich Bretzner (already set by another composer in 1781), sparked a row between the two men of letters. Bretzner threatened action over alleged plagiarism by 'a certain person by the name of Mozart' (though Bretzner's libretto had itself been inspired by the English Isaac Bickerstaffe's *The Captive*, a reminder of how English ballad opera influenced the native German mixture of speech and song). That certain person has immortalised the romantic escape of Constanze and her gallant cavalier from the harem. If Bretzner is remembered at all today, he has Mozart to thank.

Characters:
Belmonte, a Spanish gentleman *tenor*
Pedrillo, his servant *tenor*
Constanze, Belmonte's beloved *soprano*
Blonde, her maid *soprano*
Osmin, the Pasha's harem-keeper *bass*
Selim Pasha *spoken*
An old sailor *mute*

The gestation of *Die Entführung* took over a year during which Mozart took pupils, composed a little, became linked with Constanze Weber in gossip, and suffered incessantly reproachful letters from his father. The work had been intended for the visit of a Russian royal personage at the end of 1781. The visit was constantly postponed and *The Seraglio*

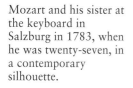

Mozart and his sister at the keyboard in Salzburg in 1783, when he was twenty-seven, in a contemporary silhouette.

finally burst on to the stage of the Burgtheater on July 16 1782. It was on this occasion that the Emperor allegedly commented, 'too many notes, dear Mozart'; to which the composer, doubtless recalling his exalted state above the cooks though below the valets, replied sharpish, 'Exactly the right number, your majesty.'

The première

Despite other tensions – the hostility of Italian singers and the musical establishment, nervous of this young composer – *Die Entführung* enjoyed a triumphant première. At the second performance Mozart noted organised hissing from some sections of the audience in Act 1, but that was drowned in the enthusiastic reception by the end. Gluck requested an extra performance, and the work's popularity quickly spread outside Vienna.

So-called 'Turkish' operas were popular in Vienna at the time. It was only a century since the Ottomans had besieged Vienna (and, when repulsed, had left bags of curious black beans behind them, thus triggering the European passion for coffee). The Turk was a colourfully entertaining stage figure, much as 'Chermans who haff vays of making you talk' have come to be laughed at in present-day sitcom: a way of assimilating yesterday's enemies (and perhaps secretly reassuring ourselves: the Viennese needed reassurance, for in the next reign war with the Turks turned from comic convention to grim reality). In Osmin, the ferocious but ineffectual overseer of the Pasha's garden, Mozart created a richly comic character, not merely a bullying villain but a clown and – even – a rather touching dupe. His very first aria sounds a sombre note of love-lorn cynicism: this man has had unhappy experiences.

At the other extreme of the vocal range, Constanze is given wonderfully varied music, ranging from tender sadness to heroic defiance. The creator of the role was Catarina Cavalieri, mistress of the composer Salieri, whose rivalry with Mozart has become legendary. Mozart the dramatist, Mozart the intuitive psychologist, is bursting to create real, rounded human beings; and in high-flying soprano and sonorous bass he looks forward to the mercurial figures who throng the stage in the operas he wrote with Lorenzo da Ponte.

If Belmonte is characterised as merely merely a 'romantic' knight-errant, his music is unfailingly elegant; the comic servants are descendants of the perky wheeler-dealers that people the popular German *Singspiel* with its spoken dialogue, glancing back at all comic servants from Plautus to *commedia dell'arte* (but as yet a world away from the dynamic Figaro and Susanna). The composer was still keeping a shrewd eye on the native German tradition. That was his brief. But he added an exotic richness to the orchestra, a theatrical flexibility from Italian comic opera, and a depth of feeling to what could have been the toy-theatre pasteboard characters, all of which place *Entführung* firmly in his 'big five' operas.

Act 1

The action takes place in seventeenth-century Turkey. Act 1 opens in the square in front of the Pasha Selim's palace, near the seashore. Belmonte, a young Spanish noblemen, arrives in search of Constanze, currently held captive by the Pasha. He pours out his feelings – hope that he can soon see his beloved and recollection of the sorrow he has suffered – in an aria that delineates his character: ardent, gallant, romantic ('Hier soll ich dich denn sehen' – Here shall I then see you).

He is interrupted by a figure both lugubrious and faintly sinister. Osmin, the Pasha's overseer, emerges to pick figs. He philosophises about the fickleness of women in a wonderfully folksy vein whose minor-key melancholy sounds a distinct note of regret and warning ('Wer ein Liebchen hat gefunden' – A man who finds a sweetheart). Eventually he deigns to notice Belmonte and bustling music expresses the young man's impatience as he tries to get information from the cantankerous official – on this showing the archetypal 'jobsworth'. Osmin is goaded to anger at the mention of Belmonte's manservant Pedrillo, also a captive, and in overlapping phrases that mockingly contradict one another Belmonte sings his praises while Osmin snarls his loathing.

Belmonte beats a retreat after this lively duet. He therefore misses Pedrillo, who indulges in lively backchat with Osmin, provoking the latter into an aria of anger: a *tour de force*, initially declamatory, then speeding up into comically angular vocal leaps until he splutters with indignation and flounces into the house to the sound of exotic Turkish-style percussion.

Belmonte returns. In the excited spoken dialogue of their reunion Pedrillo fills his master in: he, Constanze and her maid Blonde are captives of Selim Pasha. A chivalrous captor, Selim loves Constanze, who rejects him. Blonde is also being wooed by the considerably less gentlemanly Osmin. The two Spaniards plan to introduce Belmonte into the Pasha's service as an architect. Once he has gained access to the household Belmonte can arrange their escape on the ship awaiting them outside the harbour.

In a recitative and aria ('O wie ängstlich' – Oh how fearful) Belmonte expresses his excitement at the prospect of seeing Constanze again (underlined by scurrying wind and breathless string phrases in the orchestra). He hides as a procession of janissaries heralds the arrival of the Pasha and Constanze. Mozart strikes a favourite mock-Turkish note both in the chorus' melodic line and the colourful orchestration.

Constanze resists the Pasha's wooing and recalls her true love, Belmonte. The aria 'Ach, ich liebte' (How I loved) is deceptively simple: heartfelt, direct, opening with almost introspective musing and ending with a high, florid declaration of sorrow.

Selim gives Constanze another day to change her mind. After she leaves, Pedrillo succeeds in getting Belmonte taken on as an architect in the Pasha's service. The act ends with the two Spaniards attempting to enter the palace despite the resistance of Osmin – obviously the prototype of every car-park attendant, commissionaire and bank clerk who has delighted in obstructiveness for its own sake. In a brisk trio they push past the furious functionary and enter the palace.

Act 2

We meet Constanze's English maid, the improbably named Blonde, giving a lesson in love, or rather manners, to the exasperated Osmin, who persists in regarding her as his slave. In a demure little aria, all simple sweetness ('Durch Zärtlichkeit und Schmeicheln' – Through tenderness and flattery), she points out that tenderness achieves more than bullying. In the ensuing dialogue her pertness is a match for Osmin's threats. In the rollicking duet that follows Osmin warns her not to see Pedrillo and she retorts that she will not be dictated to. Osmin reflects (in a gloomy minor key, to mocking woodwind) what fools Englishmen must be to allow their womenfolk to boss them around. He finally beats a retreat at Blonde's threat to scratch his eyes out.

In dramatic contrast Constanze enters and broods on her grief. The desolate, broken-hearted phrase 'Traurigkeit' (Sorrow) raises the tone from Singspiel, and from tuppence-coloured toy theatre adventure, to serious opera. Constanze bitterly muses that she cannot (like Ilia in *Idomeneo*, we might recall) confide her grief even to the breeze since it breathes it back into her heart: conventional tragic attitudin-

Count Hieronymus
Colloredo, Bishop of
Salzburg, the arrogant
and uncomprehending
employer responsible for
Mozart's break with
Salzburg.

ising is transformed into true tragedy.

Blonde tries to cheer her mistress but the Pasha returns to warn Constanze that her day's grace is nearly over. She responds with the opera's most spectacular showpiece. 'Martern aller Artern' (Every kind of torture) is a cry of defiance that poses problems for producers, with its long orchestral prelude. What to do with the characters? Should Selim (a non-singing acting role) stay on stage, looking, it must admitted, rather superfluous, or let Constanze take the stage in a virtual concert aria? Should she be treated to a menacing array of torture implements? Should the curtain fall for the orchestral prelude to the aria, thus using it as a sort of mini-overture, with no stage business to distract?

Musically the aria is almost a concerto for voice and

orchestra, with a beautifully-written instrumental concertato effect for flute, oboe, violin and cello. After hurling defiance at the dangers that threaten her, Constanze leaves the stage with all flags flying, prepared to meet the death that will set her free.

The tension is relieved by the servants. Pedrillo breaks the news of Belmonte's arrival to an excited Blonde. In breathless dialogue he outlines an escape plan for that very night. He even has a sleeping potion for Osmin. Blonde breaks into the bubbling and high-spirited 'Welche Wonne, welche Lust' ('How delightful it will be/ When our ship sails out to sea', to quote the charming old translation by Edward J. Dent). After her departure to prepare Constanze, Pedrillo has his moment of glory. 'Frisch zum Kampe!' (Forward to the fray) inspires the orchestra to the full panoply of martial colour. The heroic tone is slightly diminished by Pedrillo's nervous reflection that only faint hearts would be afraid – to reassure himself, you suspect.

The truculent Osmin enters and Pedrillo puts his plan into action. At first the overseer rejects an invitation to share some Cyprus wine but is won over when Pedrillo cheerfully swigs his (undrugged) bottle. In a jolly duet, to a sparkingly 'Turkish'-hued accompaniment, the two men toast Bacchus, the god of wine, not to mention girls both dark and fair ('Vivat Bacchus!'). In spoken, if somewhat slurred, dialogue, Osmin, now waxing lyrical over such infidel pleasures as alcohol, is led off to sleep, leaving the coast clear for the two pairs of lovers to be reunited.

Belmonte first holds the stage with an aria of tearful joy (tender woodwind in the orchestra) with an elegantly optimistic triple-time conclusion. A duet might have been more appropriate for this tender meeting but the original tenor, Adamberger, insisted on the set number of four arias, and this patently emotional occasion obviously provided a dramatic pretext for one. This leads straight into a quartet, a foretaste of the great ensembles to come in later operas, charting the characters' changing emotions. The full heroic treatment is given to the noble couple's reunion (with a reminder of past sadness in the falling phrase of Constanze's reference to days of suffering). The bouncy excitement of below stairs intrudes on the lyrically expressed happiness of the aristocrats, and all four join in expressing jubilant hope.

The mood changes. Belmonte has a secret worry. Constanze urges him to explain, as harmonies shift ambiguously under the vocal line. While Belmonte falters out his

Mozart at twenty-nine; a silhouette of 1785.

unworthy doubts about Constanze's fidelity – has she held out against the Pasha's advances? – Pedrillo questions Blonde over her resistance to Osmin. The women respond in character: Constanze weeps, Blonde slaps Pedrillo's face. The men are at once repentant. Constanze looks to the indignant Blonde for support, much as the Countess will be consoled by the loyal Susanna after the Count's jealousy in Act 2 of *Figaro*. All four join in a theme of almost child-like simplicity associated with moralising. The men beg for pardon and the women, after some hesitation, forgive them. The act ends with a brisk hymn to love in the vein of a typical final chorus.

Act 3

But it's far from final, of course. They still have to escape, and their attempts to do so occupy the last act. In the square before the palace, with the sea, their route to safety, in the distance, Belmonte and Pedrillo arrive. The servant goes to check that all are sleeping in the palace while Belmonte addresses love in an aria ('Ich baue ganz auf deine Stärke' – I build on your strength) that sums up the grace and gallantry that characterise his music. However, as part of Adamberger's quota, it is sometimes omitted.

Pedrillo returns and gives the signal to the waiting women with an exquisite serenade – the scene is a lovely blend of dramatic urgency and sheer musical beauty. 'Im Mohrenland' (In the land of the Moors) tells the story of a knight rescuing a captive maiden, its delicately haunting quality interrupted by the anxious Belmonte. Listeners can be grateful that Pedrillo ignores his master's whispered order of 'That's enough!' and gives us two more verses. Unobserved, an old sailor sees them and goes to raise the alarm.

The women emerge; but so does a drowsy Osmin. He sees the ladder propped against the palace wall, grasps the situation and calls the guards. As the four are taken away he sings the splendid 'Ha, wie will ich triumphieren' (How I will triumph) – an outburst of crowing victory in which he looks forward to their execution with lip-smacking relish, all shot through with mock-oriental colour. Ferocious yet funny, this gleefully blood-curdling aria puts the seal on Osmin as the first of Mozart's great comic operatic creations.

The scene changes to the Pasha's apartments. In the general revelations, the Turk discovers that Belmonte is the son of the Spanish nobleman who was his arch-enemy, the man who robbed and betrayed him and stole his beloved. Belmonte admits that his father, had the positions been reversed, would have exacted a hideous revenge on the son of an old enemy. 'I see you know your father well,' observes the Pasha dryly. He leaves the captives to brood on their imminent punishment as he prepares their doom (one is irresistibly reminded of the Mikado thinking up a little something 'lingering, with boiling oil' in similar circumstances).

Belmonte and Constanze begin their recitative and duet ('Welch ein Geschick!' – What a fate) with dignity into which a note of human warmth breaks with Belmonte's cry of 'Engelsseele!'. The music's mood becomes expansive, climaxing with the lovers' glowing affirmation that they want only to stay together ('Ach, Geliebte' – Ah, beloved). They face their fate together in rapture, expressed in music more conventionally florid and heroic.

Their servants join them. The four are resigned to the worst when the Pasha appears; he puts them to shame by explaining that he despises Belmonte's father too much to follow his example. Belmonte and Constanze are free to go. This is a more moving – and less far-fetched – version of Brietzner's original dénouement, the discovery that Belmonte was the long-lost son of Selim himself. It's also more in keeping with the rational humanism of the enlightenment that so appealed to Mozart.

To Osmin's fury, Pedrillo and Blonde are also freed. The finale is modelled on a traditional 'vaudeville' where each character has his or her say in turn with a verse, each followed by a general refrain. The noble lovers express their gratitude to the equally noble Turk. Pedrillo reflects on how close he came to being throttled. And Blonde can't resist getting in a final jibe at Osmin. Only the overseer interrupts the formal musical pattern with a typical frenzy of bloodthirsty rage, complete with drums and cymbals, as he rushes off discomfited. The four escapees from the harem sing a final tribute to mercy, and the chorus of janissaries rounds off this baroque glimpse of eastern magic with a final splash of exotic local colour.

Chapter 4

Two Fragments, a Comedy and a Wedding: *The Marriage of Figaro*

Given the command of the operatic form that Mozart had shown in *The Seraglio* – not to mention its popular success – it is surprising that we have to wait four years for his next large-scale opera, though no surprise that it is the supreme masterpiece of the Mozart canon, and perhaps of the whole operatic repertory.

The intervening years were eventful, personally and professionally. Amadé married his Constanze after a slight awkwardness with her mother, who made him sign a contract promising financial payment if he refused – shades of Figaro and Marcellina! They started a family, though their first child, Raimund Leopold, died as a baby. Mozart became a Freemason; he reached the height of his fame and success as a pianist as well as a composer, as witness his output of piano concertos and the six string quartets dedicated to an appreciative Haydn. Musical and social life happily overlapped at quartet parties, such as the one in 1784 recalled by the Irish tenor Michael Kelly, where the violins were played by Haydn and Dittersdorf; the composer Vanhal played the cello while Mozart took the viola part.

Mozart's reputation went far beyond Vienna. In 1783 a Hamburg paper used his name as a gauge of success when prophesying that a thirteen-year-old pianist could become 'a second Mozart' (the thirteen-year-old was called Beethoven). During this period Amadé even ventured back to his unloved home town, half-fearing he would be arrested (technically he was still in the employ of the archbishop; his departure had been, to put it politely, informal). Even big sister Nannerl finally married, making a good match with a local Salzburg bigwig. But – an ominous foretaste of problems to come –

Mozart began to borrow money. For all Amadé's success, the couple were already living beyond their means; and his health began to suffer.

Meanwhile he continued to hanker after a suitable opera libretto. When commissioned by the court theatre to do an Italian opera in the wake of *The Seraglio's* success, Mozart claimed to look through a hundred libretti without finding one that would not require so many changes as to make it hardly worthwhile. He had by this time met an unfrocked priest, a certain Abbate da Ponte, who had promised a new libretto, but Mozart suspected he might be in league with rival composers such as Salieri. In despair the composer even turned to the Salzburg court chaplain, that Abbé Varesco who had angrily demanded more money for all the extra work he put into *Idomeneo*.

The Goose of Cairo

However, Varesco's theatrical shortcomings in opera seria were as nothing compared with his misguided touch in comedy. *L'oca del Cairo* (The Goose of Cairo) deals with two unwilling fiancées escaping from unwanted marriages with the help of their lovers and the usual sprightly conniving servants. The court chaplain's imagination extended to a second act climax with a huge mechanical goose; and here Mozart, not surprisingly, balked. The work exists in fragment form. Half-a-dozen numbers exist with vocal line, instrumental bass part and other instrumental indications, and attempts have been made to salvage a performable whole, starting with a concert performance in Frankfurt in 1860. An arrangement, with numbers from *Lo sposo deluso* (see below), was performed in Paris in 1867, a one-act adaptation was staged in London in 1940, and New York saw it in 1953 as *Don Pedros Heimkehr* (Don Pedro's Homecoming) in a version that incorporated other numbers. The English composer Stephen Oliver produced a version for the Battignano Festival in 1991.

Of *Lo sposo deluso* (The Deluded Husband) only five numbers survive. Thwarted matrimonial plans, amorous cross-purposes and a dash of satirised snobbery make up a plot that some have attributed to da Ponte, though it's probably a hack reworking of Cimarosa's earlier *Le donne rivali*. The most significant thing in the score is the allocation, in Mozart's handwriting, of various singers to the characters – the singers of the new Italian company which would eventually perform *Figaro*.

Der Schauspieldirektor

If the chance to write a successful Italian comic opera continued to elude Mozart, he found an opportunity to compose a short German comedy. By direct request of the Emperor, *Der Schauspieldirektor* (The Impresario) was performed at the Orangerie in the Schönbrunn Palace on February 7 1786. It was part of a double bill about the headaches of operatic creativity; at the other end of the hall Salieri's *Prima la musica poi le parole* (Music First, Words Afterwards) followed Mozart, in front of a court audience that included the governor-general of the Netherlands. The words of the comedy were by Gottlieb Stephanie, Mozart's librettist for *The Seraglio*, who evidently identified with the character of Frank, the put-upon and harassed entrepreneur of the title.

The wretched man (a spoken role) finds himself between two rival sopranos, each claiming the right to the higher fee. Mme Herz's speciality is limpid tear-jerking, Mme Silberklang indulges in dazzling vocal acrobatics (lovely wind accompaniment). Each has a display piece that bombards the impresario (and the audience) with its brilliance. Other singing characters include Buff, a comic singer, and Monsieur Vogelsang, the tenor, who also gets dragged into the competition. Only when the exasperated Frank threatens to throw up the whole enterprise do the rivals realise the importance of pulling together, and the little work ends with a philosophical vaudeville.

For all its jolly triviality the work contains gems, starting with the overture, rightly a concert piece in its own right, and including the trio where the singers try to out-do each other. Mozart's work is still performed as a curtain-raiser, Salieri's is virtually forgotten (though it was revived in Spitalfields in 1995); yet the Italian was paid twice as much as the Austrian.

Lorenzo Da Ponte

By this time Mozart had already started on the composition of *Figaro*. Unlike the creative process of *Idomeneo*, the birth-pangs of this masterpiece are not documented in voluminous correspondence. We depend mainly on Lorenzo Da Ponte's memoirs, published 40 years later, for an account of the genesis of the work, but the idea of setting Beaumarchais' daring new play *La folle journée, ou le mariage de Figaro* seems to have been Mozart's. The comedy's revolutionary overtones have perhaps been exaggerated by commentators, or maybe in hindsight the class tensions between the masters and servants, privilege and dependence struggling for dignity, have

Lorenzo Da Ponte, adventurer, librettist and first professor of Italian in New York.

been thrown into sharper relief than intended by what came after, almost as if the play were heralding the French Revolution.

Certainly the depiction of the lord as outwitted by his servant and begging pardon from his wife was refreshingly novel; but the satire in the original was aimed more at the legal system than at overweening aristocrats. Still, the play was considered sufficiently outspoken and potentially shocking – by Viennese standards – to have been banned from the Viennese stage by the censor at the behest, it appears, of the Emperor himself. Even the reforming Joseph II considered the comedy contained 'much that is objectionable'.

But Da Ponte, poet, author and adventurer with a dash of his compatriot Casanova about him, was in his element among the schemes and intrigues of Vienna, and he himself allegedly won the Emperor, however unwittingly, round to the idea that 'what cannot be said may be sung', as one contemporary newspaper put it. The Venetian Da Ponte ended a long life (he died at nearly ninety in 1838) as the first professor of Italian at Columbia University. His memoirs are gamey

Michael Kelly: tenor, raconteur and Dublin wine merchant.

and sometimes wildly self-romanticised, to be taken with a large pinch of salt but eminently readable. See his famous account of his working method, for example, when he was writing libretti for several composers (including Salieri as well as Mozart) at the same time, aided by a bottle of wine and 'a pretty sixteen-year-old (whom I had wished to love only as a daughter, but . . .' . The girl would come to the sound of a bell 'which, to be truthful, rang a great deal: she fetched me now a biscuit, now a cup of coffee, now nothing but her own pretty face, fashioned to arouse poetic inspiration.'

Michael Kelly, the Irish tenor who ended up as a wine-merchant in Dublin, has also left his memoirs. He recalls that even once the opera was completed, much manoeuvring was necessary to get the go-ahead for its production in front of rival works by composers such as Righini. The Emperor's personal decision that *Figaro* should take precedence may have been the result of his satisfaction with *The Impresario*.

Figaro premièred

On May 1 1786 *Le nozze di Figaro* had its première at the Burgtheater. The role of Susanna was taken by Nancy Storace, a British soprano for whom Mozart may have had a certain tenderness: the piano part in the concert aria 'Ch'io mi scordi di te', composed at about this time, and performed with Mozart at the piano, supports the voice like a suitor; the aria may be a secret declaration of love. The applause during the performance and the demand for encores meant that the work ran for nearly twice as long as expected and resulted in an official ban on encores thereafter. The composer received a flat fee of 450 gulden, as much as a concert would have earned him, with no prospect of royalties or further earnings.

Characters:
Count Almaviva *baritone*
Figaro, his valet *bass-baritone*
Countess Almaviva *soprano*
Susanna, her maid, Figaro's fiancée *soprano*
Cherubino, a pageboy *soprano/mezzo-soprano*
Bartolo *bass*
Marcellina, a housekeeper *soprano/mezzo-soprano*
Don Basilio, a music teacher *tenor*
Antonio, a gardener *baritone*
Barbarina, his daughter *soprano*
Don Curzio, a lawyer *tenor*

Nancy Storace: the first Susanna in *The Marriage of Figaro*, at the age of twenty-one, and possibly more than just a colleague to Mozart.

Figaro is a summer opera, from the freshly-gathered flowers the village girls strew before their noble patrons to the pine-scented midnight garden where, as in the Forest of Arden in *As You Like It*, the tangles of love, pain and forgiveness are sorted out and every Jack has his Jill in an almost ritualistic resolution that lifts the mundane to a near-mystic level. In a good stage production of the last act you can almost smell the warmth of the southern night in what is arguably one of the greatest musical expressions of affection, family ties and (whisper it not to Wagner fans) erotic love.

A good production can also choose to underline the social tensions, the hint of revolution in the air; but the political aspects of Beaumarchais' original play (in any case satirising the legal system rather than the nobility) have been subsumed into the corresponding emotional and sexual antagonisms, adding a dimension to the outraged masculine pride of those sparring partners, the Count Almaviva and his valet Figaro.

Act 1

The overture plunges straight into the scurrying bustle of plot and counter-plot that make up the 'crazy day' of Beaumarchais' original title. It fizzes to a giddy stop and the curtain rises on a partly furnished room in Aguas Frescas, the Count's country mansion. Figaro, the Count's manservant, is measuring the floor, giving little attention to his fiancée Susanna, the Countess's maid, as she fusses in front of the mirror with her home-made wedding bonnet.

The busy, cheerful little duet, Susanna jokingly cross at Figaro's inattention, her fiancé preoccupied by his task, is followed by recitative in which Susanna is mysteriously disturbed to learn that this is the room the Count has allocated to the couple as their nuptial bedroom. In a duettino ('Se a caso Madama' – Should my lady call you) Figaro explains how conveniently situated it is to answer the call of their employers. Susanna replies darkly that this is precisely the trouble. The tone of good-natured badinage subtly changes as Figaro's suspicions are aroused.

In recitative Susanna reveals that the Count has been making advances to her. He has even used Don Basilio, the seedy singing teacher, as a go-between. Even the dowry which the Count has promised his employee depends on her cooperation; almost as if he wanted to restore that old feudal privilege that gave the local lord the right to enjoy a bride from his estates on the night of her wedding. The legendary *'jus primae noctis'* (right of the first night) may well be a

Canone à 4 Voci.

Vienna. the 24 april. 1787.

Don't never forget your true and faithfull friend

Wolfgang Amadè Mozart

A memento to an English friend – perhaps Nancy Storace's composer brother, Stephen.

myth; it had not existed in civilised Europe for centuries, and certainly not even in *ancien régime* France, but its threat hangs over the action of *Figaro* as a symbol of outrageous privilege. It is as well to remember that such privilege existed as much in Mozart's Vienna as in pre-Revolutionary France, and the audience would have known, for all the comedy, that unjustified privilege was being challenged.

Left alone, Figaro reflects sardonically on the Count's scheme to seduce Susanna. The mood of his aria ('Se vuol ballare' – if you want to dance) is playful but dangerous. If the Count dances it will be to Figaro's tune; he can teach his master a new step or two. The straightforward mockery in three-four rhythm leads to an angrier middle section in double time where Figaro, his mask of laughter dropping, swears to sabotage the Count's plans.

A pair of schemers

After his departure another pair of schemers bustles in: Bartolo, an old doctor and former guardian of the Countess (whom he desired for himself before her elopement with the Count), and Marcellina, the housekeeper. The latter has been explaining that she lent Figaro money with a contract that stipulated marriage between them if he defaulted (did Mozart remember his mother-in-law, Mme Weber, with her similar document on behalf of her daughter? Constanze tore it up in embarrassment, but the memory must have rankled). He has still to pay her and now, on the day fixed for Figaro's wedding to Susanna, she hopes to break up the happy couple. Bartolo, remembering the part Figaro played in aiding the

Almavivas' elopement, looks forward to vengeance in a pompously self-important aria ('La vendetta') with a patter section of Gilbert and Sullivan relish in which he reels off the legalistic tricks he can use.

He leaves Marcellina. Her encounter with the returning Susanna is marked by a duet of feline courtesies and exaggerated politeness. Only when Susanna pointedly refers, with mock reverence, to her rival's age, does Marcellina lose her temper and flounce out.

The next arrival is Cherubino, the pageboy, his adolescent head spinning with thoughts of love. As usual he's in a scrape: the Count has dismissed him; perhaps his godmother the Countess, on whom he has a crush, can intercede for him. Cherubino pours out his heart in an aria 'Non so più' (I can't tell) that evokes the tremulous excitement of adolescence as the boy breathlessly describes his mood-swings, longings he can't define. Love obsesses him, sleeping or waking, and if nobody will listen to him he'll talk about love to mountains, flowers, fountains . . . or simply himself. Cherubino is the first of the great *travesti* parts, male roles played by women, *Hosenrollen* or trouser-roles, which succeeded the castrato tradition and which would last into our own century with Octavian, for example, in Strauss' *Der Rosenkavalier*.

Eavesdropping

This enchanting diagnosis of puberty with its throbbing orchestral accompaniment is followed by the arrival of the Count himself. In a panic the page hides behind an easy-chair, only to hear his master press his attentions on the doubly-embarrassed Susanna. The Count is in his turn embarrassed by a new arrival, the sleazy Don Basilio, music master, meddler and incurable scandal-monger. The Count hides behind the chair while the page, still unseen, in the nick of time darts round the front and is concealed by a dress Susanna quickly throws over the chair.

In the circumstances Basilio could hardly do worse than launch into gossip about the household – including the sheep's eyes that the page-boy makes at the Countess; everybody's talking about it. This is too much for the Count, who reveals himself, to Basilio's secret delight. The ensuing trio depicts Susanna's embarrassment, her resort to a pretended swoon, and a quick avoidance of the chair with its hidden eavesdropper as the men solicitously guide her to it. The sly, sliding harmonies for the male voices reflect the lecherous eagerness with which the men fondle the apparently faint girl,

The great comic bass Salvatore Baccaloni as Dr Bartolo in the pre-war Glyndebourne *Marriage of Figaro*.

the Count forgetting his anger and Basilio his Uriah Heep-like unctuousness. Inevitably, during the course of this tricky manoeuvring, the Count lifts the dress from the chair and, to his fury, sees the terrified Cherubino crouched there. In the trio's final refrain he turns angrily on Susanna while Basilio hugs himself with glee.

The Count reluctantly calms down when he realises that Cherubino overheard his advances to his wife's maid. The tense situation is interrupted by the entrance of Figaro, a wedding veil in his hands, and the villagers, who scatter flowers before their lord. In a gracefully pastoral chorus they pointedly refer to the chaste flower that the Count allows them to preserve. Figaro has evidently set the little scene up, an opportunity for him to ask for his master to let the wedding take place at once. The Count delays, hoping to find Marcellina and accordingly halt the wedding completely.

The villagers depart, leaving the disappointed couple and the crestfallen Cherubino with the Count. The page-boy artlessly promises not to repeat what he overheard while hidden behind the chair, and the nobleman, angry and embarrassed, commutes his punishment to a commission in the Count's own regiment. After the Count leaves, Figaro sardonically bids the boy farewell in the mock-martial strains of 'Non più andrai' (No more roaming), perhaps the most famous aria in the score: no more gadding about like an amorous butterfly, no more dandified clothes; a warrior's life calls, marching through mud, bullets flying, plenty of glory but not much money. The curtain falls to the sound of a march as poor Cherubino renounces the boudoir for the barracks.

Act 2

Act 2 introduces us to the mistress of the house. The Countess is pining in her apartments. In a limpidly plaintive aria ('Porgi Amor' – Vouchsafe, O love) she implores the god of love to restore her husband's affections to her. The Countess is something of a puzzle. In her previous incarnation as Rosina in Beaumarchais' *The Barber of Seville*, she was a spirited girl who was full of gumption and knew her own mind. Heartbreak at the philandering of the dashing young cavalier she eloped with so joyfully has unnerved her. One producer (Johannes Schaaf at Covent Garden) has even made her an alcoholic. Another (Jonathan Miller, English National Opera) gave her children as a way of filling out recent history and explaining her apparent lack of achievement. Her music has a certain languid resignation, but she can rouse herself from wistfulness to determination, as we shall see in her Act 3 aria; and the last solo words in the opera belong, crucially, to her.

Susanna and later Figaro join her, upstairs and downstairs combining in a plot to make the Count look foolish. Figaro has sent the Count an anonymous note alleging an assignation between the Countess and a lover. The Count's search for this imaginary rival should keep him out of mischief until he has no further excuse to delay Figaro's wedding. As a *coup de grace*, to force his noble master's hand once and for all, Figaro decides to have the Count lured into the garden with

The enchanting pre-war soprano Lotte Schoene not looking excessively masculine as a rather principal-boy Cherubino.

the promise of meeting Susanna, only to find a decoy – Cherubino, say, dressed as a girl. The Countess could then surprise her husband in the act of philandering and embarrass him into letting the servants' wedding go ahead.

Figaro bounces off to fetch Cherubino, who shyly allows himself to be disguised. His calf-love for the Countess is much in evidence, and, after prompting, he sings a little song he has written – about love, naturally. Susanna accompanies the charming 'Voi che sapete' (You ladies who know) on the guitar. With its fragile delicacy mirrored in the orchestra (woodwind, pizzicato strings), the song is a more controlled version of his amorous outburst in Act 1. Trembling, blushing, hot and cold, he languishes in uncertainty, but rather enjoys it. Is this love?

Left to right: Lisa Della Casa (Countess), Mildred Miller (Cherubino) and the inimitable Viennese soprano Irmgard Seefried (Susanna) in a New York Metropolitan Opera production of *The Marriage of Figaro*.

Cherubino dresses up

Locking the door, the Countess and Susanna begin to dress Cherubino as a girl as part of the plot against the Count. Amidst much playful teasing, the Countess notices that the boy's military commission hasn't yet been sealed – a detail that will later become important as the plot thickens.

Susanna makes Cherubino kneel as she begins to disguise him. The little aria 'Venite, inginocchiatevi' (Come here and kneel before me), often overlooked in performance because of the comic stage business, provides one of those moments of sheer musico-theatrical rightness which drop into Mozart's lap directly from heaven. Susanna comments on the page's prettiness and in a refrain remarks that women will have good reason to fall in love with him. The words are 'Se l'amano le femmine, han certo il lor perchè' ('If women all go mad for him, they'll have good reason why,' to quote the charmingly apt old Dent translation). The music concerned is a delightful theme, but Mozart adds a dash of magic by dropping an octave in mid-phrase: the expected note comes

out in a lower register than expected, the perfect musical equivalent of a chuckle, a knowing nudge in the ribs, as Susanna – and Mozart – turn to us and wink.

The by-play between Cherubino and the Countess turns into delicate, unadmitted flirtation. The original play's audience would certainly have expected some sort of relationship between the two, and the playwright Beaumarchais duly obliged – the third in the trilogy of Figaro plays is called *La Mère Coupable* – the guilty mother – and deals with the love-child of the Countess and Cherubino. The bubbling innocence of the page-boy in Mozart's opera should not be confused with the daintiness of a Dresden figurine. This is a hot-blooded adolescent.

Susanna goes to her room to fetch a ribbon. Just as the Countess is consoling the emotional youth, a knock is heard. Her husband is back from the hunt unexpectedly early; panic ensues. The Countess bundles the boy into her dressing-room and locks him in before admitting her husband. She is flustered, he is suspicious, especially after a crash is heard from the dressing-room. The Countess claims that Susanna is trying on her wedding-dress in there.

Enter the Count

As the Count raps on the door and commands her to come out, Susanna enters from her own room on the other side of the stage and, grasping the situation, quickly hides. The trio that follows – menacing Count, distressed Countess, Susanna in dismayed asides – crystallises the different emotions in a beautifully controlled form. Time is suspended while dramatic urgency tugs at these characters – an apparent contradiction that opera manages so well and that Mozart brought to perfection.

To avoid a scandal in front of the servants, the Count will find the tools to force open the door himself, convinced that a man is hiding in his wife's dressing-room. He takes his wife with him, locking all the doors behind them.

Susanna rushes from her hiding-place and in a quick, frightened duet ('Aprite, presto, aprite' – Open, quickly open), urges Cherubino to flee. He comes out of the dressing-room in a panic: all the doors are locked, there is only one way out. The page-boy leaps from the window and for a moment the tension is replaced by sheer relief as Susanna watches him hare off into the distance. She recollects herself and takes his place in the dressing-room. Mischievously she declares herself ready for the bullying Count.

The Count and Countess return; he is ready to break the door down and kill any man he finds. In a desperate attempt to calm her husband, the Countess decides to tell him the truth. She and Susanna were preparing a trick, a harmless prank, together with . . . Cherubino. The Count's anger at coming across the troublesome boy yet again is frightening. As he bangs furiously on the dressing-room door, it's as well to remember that, for all the situation's farcical overtones, the Count is deadly serious. If Cherubino, or any man, were in his wife's dressing-room, the Count would unhesitatingly, and with impunity, kill him.

The Act 2 finale which now begins is one of the marvels of musico-theatrical architecture: twenty minutes of music perfectly portraying the rapidly changing emotions in a multi-layered drama, with brilliant psychological insight and immaculately judged changes of pace. The plot charges on with convoluted twists, bluff, double-bluff, rage, fear, guilt, love, hate and comic confusion – plus a dash of unexpected drunken low comedy.

Geraint Evans (Figaro) and Ilva Ligabue (Countess) at Covent Garden.

The following scene is one of the glories of opera. It begins with the Count calling Cherubino out with an angry, emphatic phrase ('Esci ormai, garzon malnato' – Out you come, wretched boy). The Countess pleads for mercy, her music writhing with anxiety and embarrassment. There follows her faltering confession that the boy may be in a state of undress – it was purely to disguise him as a woman, she assures her husband. The Count's rage is implacable and unyielding while her fluttering vocal line conveys her panic.

The Count goes to the dressing-room door. To his amazement – and the Countess's – out trips Susanna to music suddenly demure and tongue-in-cheek. Here's the villain, says Susanna, as the music adds its own dimension of wide-eyed mock-innocence. Both husband (baffled) and wife (baffled but relieved) express their surprise as Susanna chortles to herself.

Susanna explains

Still suspicious, the Count blusters into the dressing-room to see for himself. Susanna quickly explains matters to the Countess, and both women are ready to punish the Count when he comes out, non-plussed and even – for him – apologetic. The Countess, only half joking, strikes a reproachful pose. Susanna consoles her mistress, snapping at the Count when he turns to her for help. To increasingly confident music that now begins to chug perkily along, the women assert that the whole thing was a joke to tease him; as was the anonymous letter about an assignation, which they admit was written by Figaro.

In a typical heart-touching moment, the bustling music of comic bluff and explanation, mock-indignation and genuine bewilderment, modulates into a radiant confirmation of forgiveness on all sides. The Count repents, the women ruefully admit that men were always, will always be, like this.

The tenderness between the Almavivas is abruptly interrupted by Figaro, cheerfully announcing the musicians and wedding guests. The Count's annoyance at the anonymous letter returns. The bucolically cheerful triple-time takes on an ominously insistent rhythm, as gently menacing as a time-bomb ticking, while the Count senses another excuse to put off the wedding.

To brisker, more straightforward music, the Count questions Figaro about the letter. Unaware that the two women have revealed the hoax, the valet feigns ignorance, to the irritation of the women who prompt him to tell the truth. The comedy must end, urges the company impatiently, a neat cue for him to ask the Count to end it in the traditional manner – with a wedding. The Countess joins the engaged couple in begging the Count's permission for the marriage to take place; like a shaft of sunlight falling across the scene, by a Mozartian sleight-of-hand their music takes on a radiant, almost hymn-like quality, while the Count's vocal line grumbles angrily underneath.

The seductive Act III duet for the Count and Susanna, tried out by Mozart and Michael Kelly when just composed (according to Kelly's entertaining memoirs).

A pot of carnations

Suddenly in bursts Antonio, the gardener, brandishing a broken pot of carnations. Mood and music change abruptly to express comic chaos: his anger, the puzzled irritation of the others. He announces that a man has leapt down from the balcony into his flowers. The Count is suddenly alert. The women turn helplessly to Figaro, who plays for time by commenting on the gardener's drunkenness and – a desperate inspiration – finally claims that he was the one who jumped. In snarling tit-for-tat repartee between Antonio and Figaro, the gardener mentions the page-boy: the company is thrown on to the alert again but Figaro improvises nobly, spinning a yarn about waiting for Susanna, panicking at the sound of the Count's voice, impulsively leaping from the window . . . He even, like Gilbert and Sullivan's Pooh-Bah, adds 'corroborative detail to give artistic verisimilitude to an otherwise bald and unconvincing narrative' by feigning a sprained foot.

The change to a prowling Andante in six-eight time heralds a return to time-bomb mode as Antonio produces papers dropped by the escaper. The Count seizes them before Figaro can see them. To the women's *sotto voce* (and doubtless infuriating) urgings to think quickly, Figaro is cross-examined by his suspicious master. The ruthlessly throbbing triple-time continues under Antonio's dismissal (he and Figaro exchange insults to the last) like a nervous tic in Figaro's head as he plays for time.

The Countess gets a glimpse of the document: it's Cherubino's commission. The women manage to whisper it to Figaro who, brilliant actor that he is, seems suddenly to remember. Of course, he tells the Count, it is the page's commission!

What was Figaro doing with it? demands his master relentlessly. The Countess, remembering, whispers to Susanna who passes it on to her fiancé: it needed sealing. Figaro triumphantly parries the Count's interrogation. Unable to catch his servant out, the Count rages quietly while the three conspirators join in hushed, cautious jubilation – fingers crossed. It looks as though they can survive the storm.

But nothing is that simple. The door bursts open (*allegro assai*) and in march Marcellina, Bartolo and Basilio, the Count's tawdry allies, with their bombshell: insistence on Figaro's repayment of his debt to Marcellina or marriage to her as agreed. Three assertive statements each dissolve into triumphant patter. The fastest music ends the act in traditional comic confusion. Figaro, Susanna and the Countess lament the latest hitch; the Count and his acolytes crow in delight. The fizzing *prestissimo* sets a hilarious seal on the brilliant, tightly-constructed and unstoppable twenty-minute kaleidoscope; and brings down the curtain on Act 2.

Act 3

A reception hall in the palace. In recitative the Count broods on the day's events. He knows something is not quite right and it piques both his personal vanity and his sense of honour.

In the background the Countess and Susanna enter, unseen by the Count. At her mistress' bidding the maid has come to entrap the master. As the Countess withdraws, Susanna coquettishly inflames the Count and they launch into an enchanting duet in which Susanna agrees to a rendezvous with the Count for that night. In her nervousness she sometimes gives the wrong answer to his urgent demands: she will come? he asks; yes of course. She won't fail? No. She'll come this evening? No. *No?* he snaps; yes, of course, she hastily corrects herself. She ruefully excuses herself to the audience as the Count exults at the prospect of the evening's pleasure.

The tenor Michael Kelly, who doubled as Basilio and Curzio in the original cast, recalled in his memoirs how he and a light-hearted Mozart were the first to try out the little duet together. 'I called on him one evening; he said to me, "I have just finished a little duet for my opera, you shall hear it." He sat down to the piano, and we sang it. . . . A more delicious morceau never was penned by man, and it has often been a source of pleasure to me, to have been the first who heard it, and to have sung it with its greatly gifted composer.'

Kelly also gives a glimpse of the composer at rehearsal, 'with his crimson pelisse and gold-laced cocked hat', conducting Figaro's aria at the end of Act 1. 'The effect was electricity itself, for the whole of the performers on the stage, as if actuated by one feeling of delight, vociferated Bravo! Bravo! Maestro. Viva, viva, grande Mozart. Those in the orchestra I thought would never have ceased applauding, by beating the bows of their violins against the music desks. The little man acknowledged, by repeated obeisances, his thanks for the distinguished mark of enthusiastic applause bestowed upon him.'

As Susanna leaves, with some relief, she meets Figaro. While they hurry away, her whispered remark that they have as good as won is overheard by the Count. In a magnificent recitative and aria of anger and outraged pride, he rails against the indignity of being outwitted by servants. A splendid mixture of social and sexual combativeness, the aria leaves no doubt that the man is an aristocrat and accordingly dangerous. Try to outwit him and you play with fire. The orchestral accompaniment surges with menacing bravado as he addresses himself to revenge.

The gardener's daughter, Barbarina, scampers in with Cherubino. The page should have left by now but his rustic sweetheart (who has also caught the Count's eye) persuades him to stay for the wedding: as a joke she can disguise him as one of the girls presenting flowers to the Countess. You might think Cherubino has had enough of such pranks, but they trot off happily.

The Countess's solo scene is customarily played now, after years of following the reconciliation sextet. There are historical arguments for this, but musically and dramatically too the relocation works well. Nervous at tricking an impetuous and jealous husband, in a long accompanied recitative the Countess reflects bitterly on the humiliation of being reduced to scheming with her servant.

The aria 'Dove sono' (Where are the beautiful moments?)

begins nostalgically as she recalls her past happiness and her husband's oaths of undying love. The pace quickens as she wonders whether her faithfulness and unshaken devotion could win him back. The aria ends on a note of optimistic determination.

A legal showdown

We now move to the legal showdown. Don Curzio, a lawyer traditionally played with a stammer (Michael Kelly maintains in his memoirs that he carried this over from the recitative to the sung part, improbably, in view of the precision required to observe the written score) urges Figaro to pay up or marry Marcellina. The Count is delighted. Desperately procrastinating, Figaro claims he cannot marry without his parents' consent. In response to sceptical queries he admits he knows nothing about them; he was stolen as a child. Bartolo and Marcellina show a sudden interest, and when Figaro describes a certain birthmark the revelation is complete: they are his parents.

The sextet that now follows was allegedly Mozart's own favourite number from the opera. The old couple embrace their long-lost son to a theme of calm joyfulness while the Count and lawyer mutter in frustration. Susanna enters and is promptly met by the sight of her fiancé hugging the housekeeper. She clouts him, to the admiration of her new in-laws-to-be who see this as a proof of love. Marcellina explains the situation to the sceptical girl whose repeated queries of 'sua madre?' and 'suo padre?' to the assembled company gradually turn from incredulity to delight. The ensemble ends with the two couples blissful at this unexpected family reunion while the Count and the lawyer seethe with fury and finally stalk off.

Still breathless with joy, the others decide on a double wedding – Bartolo will do the right thing by his housekeeper – and Figaro's money problems evaporate. As they leave arm in arm to tell the Countess the four declare their happiness – and mischievously add that the Count can lump it. That increasingly harassed nobleman now reappears with Antonio and is even more exasperated to hear that Cherubino is still around.

The stage is left clear for the Countess and her maid to write a letter of assignation to the Count. In fact the Countess herself will keep it, disguised as Susanna, and shame her husband publicly. In the letter duet 'Sull'aria' (How gentle the breeze) the Countess dictates and Susanna writes, echoing her mistress's phrases, until their voices entwine in a sensual evocation of a summer night. How sweet the evening breezes are, runs the cryptic message, in the pine-wood . . . . The rest he'll understand, they agree, the Countess sad, Susanna sympathetic but secretly elated that things are now coming to a head.

Led by Barbarina, the village girls bring flowers to her ladyship. She is struck by a shy, gawky figure that looks vaguely familiar. When the Count and the gardener stalk in and unmask Cherubino, the Countess is as annoyed as her husband. His rage, however, turns to embarrassment as

Disguises, bluff and double-bluff: the last act of *The Marriage of Figaro* reaches its dénouement.

Barbarina, employing what amounts to blackmail with apparent naiveté, claims Cherubino as the price for past caresses from the Count. After some thrust and parry with Figaro, the beleaguered nobleman, still sure that some plot is afoot, allows the sound of a distant march to cue the wedding festivities at last. The Almavivas, icily estranged, take their places for the double ceremony.

The celebration begins with two peasant girls singing the Count's praises with not entirely suitable sweet simplicity. As Susanna kneels before him she slips her master the letter written at the Countess' dictation. While the company dances a fandango the Count surreptitiously opens the letter. It has been sealed with a pin which, as he fumbles, pricks his finger. While dancing, Figaro observes this (though unaware who the note is from) and mockingly comments on this mysterious billet-doux to Susanna who, needless to say, wisely holds her peace. In recitative the Count announces the festivities, feasting and a ball. The chorus repeats its song of praise. The curtain falls on Figaro's wedding. But there remains much unfinished business to the marriage of Figaro.

Act 4

The pine-scented garden, later that night. By the light of the lantern, little Barbarina is searching for something and laments losing it in a plaintively lilting cavatina. Figaro and his mother enter and Barbarina artlessly reveals that she has dropped the pin that the Count is sending to Susanna as a sign of their forthcoming tryst.

She scampers off, leaving the bridegroom thunderstruck by his new wife's sudden duplicity. Marcellina tries to calm her son: she believes in Susanna – and even if the girl were guilty, she confides to the audience after the shattered Figaro has departed, she would side with her daughter-in-law anyway, as a token of solidarity against the oppressor, man.

Marcellina's aria reflects on how much better animals are at peaceful sexual coexisting than humans (evidently she is not like the visitors to London parks who write to the national press about the behaviour of the ducks in the mating season). Her complaint about the treacherous male of the human species might be termed the only dull work in the whole miraculous score and is usually omitted in performance. It may fill out the portrait of Marcellina, but hardly carries the action forward at a late stage in the proceedings as the plot is nearing its climax. Musically its florid runs, ideally demanding ease in the soprano range in a role usually cast as a mezzo, are hard to bring off for a supporting singer (one recording actually gives the aria to Susanna). And the opera's sheer length makes this belated soliloquy by a minor character something of a luxury.

In the midnight garden

The midnight garden is full of comings and goings. Having purloined some goodies from the wedding feast, Barbarina is looking for Cherubino: she escapes into a pavilion as the embittered Figaro enters with a dark lantern. He accosts Bartolo and Basilio and promises them a juicy scandal – his wife yielding to his lordship. He rushes off to prepare for the showdown, leaving Basilio the chance to philosophise. His wistful little aria, like Marcellina's usually cut in performance, reveals the human and rather touching face of the slimy go-between. He recounts, in fable form, how he has worn an ass's skin all his life to deflect danger, shame and humiliation.

Figaro returns to an empty stage. In a long accompanied recitative he pours out his grief and disillusionment at Susanna's apparent unfaithfulness. He then launches into the great 'Aprite un po' quegli occhi' (Just open those eyes), an aria that warns men not to be taken in by women's wiles. These angels are devils, they lure us like sirens, they use their charms – and the vocal line drops to a confidential tone on the words 'il resto nol dico' (the rest I pass over) – they're dazzling flirts (the rest we'll pass over), brilliant comets (the rest we'll pass over) . . . .

This cry of outraged masculinity is the answer to the Count's haughty Act 2 aria, but here a direct, conversational style takes the place of aristocratic bravura, underlining the fact that Figaro's pain stems from bruised love, not offended vanity. This is a man warning other men, his wound still fresh. The aria reaches its climax with a pun as international as it is timeless: the orchestra contributes its own jauntily mocking comment with a cheeky phrase from the horns, symbol (in different forms) of the cuckold.

This placing of Figaro's aria is the traditional one, though the conductor and musicologist John Eliot Gardiner has recently put forward the theory that the outburst is a reaction against Susanna's exquisite 'Deh vieni', that declaration of love which the eavesdropping Figaro believes is aimed at the Count and which Susanna, quite aware of his lurking presence, deliberately couches in alluring terms. A declaration of love – but to her own husband, if only he realised it.

In the conventional running order, this aria follows Figaro's. The Countess and Susanna set up the false assignation with the Count and Susanna's 'Deh vieni, non tardar' (Then come, don't delay), sung while awaiting a lover, is redolent of love on a summer night, with its delicate woodwind writing, pizzicato strings and the chromatic sensuality of the vocal line.

Amorous cross-purposes

From now on the comedy of amorous cross-purposes works quickly to its climax. Cherubino blunders in and mistakes the Countess for Susanna, as the two women have changed clothes as part of the anti-Count plot. The page promptly makes advances, a complication the already nervous Countess could well do without. The Count interrupts them and aims a slap at Cherubino which, in the darkness, hits the lurking Figaro. The aristocrat proceeds to woo his own wife under the impression that she is her maid. He escorts her into an arbour, as completely hoodwinked as the heartbroken Figaro.

An orchestral modulation, movingly expressive of tenderness, sorrow and regret, reflects the resignation behind Figaro's decision to trap the guilty lovers ('tutto è tranquillo') in the heartbreakingly beautiful evening.

The pace quickens as Susanna mischievously calls Figaro, pretending to be the Countess. When he tells her ladyship of their respective spouses' infidelity, Susanna, annoyed at her husband's lack of faith in her, forgets to disguise her voice and Figaro realises the deception, but in his turn continues the game. To her increasing dismay he makes passionate advances to her as the Countess. In asides she expresses her fury, he his laughter and love. Susanna can bear it no more and, dropping her disguise, soundly cuffs Figaro in hurt and anger. Her laughing husband reassures her in a marvellously warm and tender melody ('Pace, pace, mio dolce tesoro') that he knew it was her all the time. Their duet of reconciliation is interrupted by the frustrated Count blundering around in the darkness; and the young couple decide to draw the comedy to a close.

Figaro loudly and passionately declares his love to the 'Countess'. The Count is stunned. In outrage he calls for weapons and summons the household to witness his wife's shame. From arbour, grove and pavilion in the heady summer night tumble various characters in comic surprise: Cherubino, Barbarina, Marcellina and, apparently, the guilty Countess, in reality Susanna still in disguise. The Count refuses the pleas for mercy for her and Figaro. Suddenly the real Countess appears with her own ironically gracious request for pardon. The company is amazed and the Count, no fool, knows when he has been beaten.

And perhaps he still loves his wife; she certainly still loves him. The music that accompanies his request for forgiveness and her gentle acceding to his plea is melting, loving and wise, almost painful in its intimacy; a private moment, no matter how many people are watching, evoking who can tell what memories. For a moment the unexpected hymn-like beauty of the Countess' phrases lift the whole farce on to a higher plane.

The final chorus brings us down to earth. Lovers and friends and – especially – respectably, if only recently, wed couples hasten to join the revelry at the marriage of Figaro and Susanna.

Chapter 5

Don Giovanni

The Marriage of Figaro enjoyed a moderate success in Vienna. Views were mixed since there was the inevitable conservative and insular element that has dogged Viennese musical opinion since music was first heard on the Danube. Considering Mozart's almost fatal loyalty to the Habsburg

Leopold Mozart in 1762, the time of his children's successful tour as prodigies.

capital, the city repaid him meanly. Even so, it must have come as a surprise to be treated like a hero when he went to Prague to conduct the opera in January 1787. There *Figaro* had been ecstatically received; there were full houses for all performances. Mozart was the toast of the town. By the time he and Constanze arrived in Prague at the invitation of Count Thun, he could write home about the ball where they danced to *Figaro* arranged for quadrilles and waltzes. 'Nothing is played, sung, blown or whistled but *Figaro*.' He returned to Vienna in February with the contract for a new opera from Bondini, manager of the Prague theatre, in his pocket. Mozart immediately turned to Da Ponte for another libretto..

That very month saw the first performance in Venice – Da Ponte's home territory – of Giuseppe Gazzaniga's opera *Don Giovanni* or *Il convitato di pietra* (The Stone Guest). There are similarities with what a few months later would emerge in Mozart's own *Don Giovanni*, notably the use of the stone statue of the murdered Commendatore as an agent of supernatural retribution; but the story of Don Juan had been familiar since the monk Tirso de Molina wrote his *Burlador de Sevilla* a century and a half earlier. Molière had based a play on the story, Gluck had composed music for a ballet on the theme.

Mozart's ripening dramatic sense added depth to the more sombre elements of the story – Da Ponte was to maintain that the composer had wanted to write an entirely serious and tragic piece with no comedy or light relief. Whoever decided on the mixture that gives the work its official designation of *dramma giocoso* (merry drama), it gave Mozart the opportunity to darken his palette; above all, the opera has a dramatic surge that is almost as unstoppable as Don Giovanni's headlong rush towards hell.

The new piece gave Amadé a welcome excuse to immerse himself in work during the summer, for his father Leopold died in May. Mozart arrived in Prague in early October to supervise the new work. The opera had been scheduled for October 14 to celebrate another Habsburg marriage but as the new piece was not ready Mozart directed a revival of *Figaro* instead.

There are legends about the rehearsals for *Don Giovanni*; most famously that Mozart left the overture to the very last minute, either tossing it off during the dress rehearsal or slogging through it in the small hours. The truth is probably somewhere in between: the midnight oil certainly burnt into the small hours, but several days in advance of the first per-

Prague, the city that took Mozart to its heart. His lodgings were on the second floor, second and third windows from the right.

formance – and doubtless made bearable by the punch that Michael Kelly tells us Mozart was so fond of. The other much repeated story is that the soprano singing the peasant girl Zerlina was either unable or unwilling to shriek in a convincingly bloodcurdling way when the Don is assailing her offstage. Mozart remedied the situation by creeping up behind Mme Bondini and goosing her. The result was gratifying.

The première

Mozart-mad Prague loved the work at its first production at the National Theatre on October 29 1787. The opera was staged in Vienna the following May when some changes were made, mainly at the suggestion of the cast. Today productions tend to take the best elements of both the Prague and Vienna versions. Most notably, the Vienna Donna Elvira gained an aria ('Mi tradì' – He betrayed me) and Don Ottavio, unable to cope with the coloratura of 'Il mio tesoro' (Console my beloved) was given 'Dalla sua pace' (My peace depends on others). Luigi Bassi, the singer who created the title-role, is said to have complained about the Don's lack of definable character. It may be a monumental case of looking a gift horse in the mouth when that horse is to baritones what Hamlet is to actors, but he had a point. Nowhere does Don Giovanni reveal his true character in an aria; nowhere does he confide in us.

There are other problems with the production: what is the time-scale? Is the action continuous, taking place within twenty-four hours? (The prosaic might object to the existence of a statue to the Commendatore, presumably erected in his lifetime.) Is Don Giovanni really a womaniser or a big bluffer? And in recent years the opera has proved an ideal stamping ground for producers to try out various approaches – Marxist, Freudian and inner-city hip leap to mind. An increasingly permissive and rational society finds it hard to be horrified at the taboos flouted by the seducer-killer – this is nothing compared with *Reservoir Dogs*, after all. This might explain the attempts in recent productions to find something equally shocking on our own terms: the Don dancing with a statue of the Madonna, for instance (Glyndebourne) or urinating on the Commendatore's coffin (English National Opera).

Characters:
Don Giovanni *bass-baritone*
Leporello, his servant *bass*
Donna Anna *soprano*
Don Ottavio, her betrothed *tenor*
The Commendatore, her father *bass*
Donna Elvira, a lady from Burgos *soprano*
Zerlina, a villager *soprano*
Masetto, her betrothed *baritone*

Act 1

The overture sets the mood for the mixture of farce and moral retribution, comedy and supernatural vengeance. The notes with which Don Giovanni's murdered victim will summon him from beyond the grave are heard briefly through the swirling murk of the orchestra. Chromatic scales slither chill-

ingly like icy fingers down the spine before the music changes mood, quivering with cheeky wit and high spirits.

The overture leads into the first scene without a break. Leporello, Don Giovanni's servant, is keeping watch outside the house of Donna Anna – we'll soon find out why – and grumbling about the life his master leads him. The servant puts up with working all hours, bad food, bad pay and waiting around in the cold while his master is 'inside with a beauty'. What exactly his master's tactics are is revealed when he runs in, his face concealed, attempting to get away from Donna Anna, who clings to him while calling for help. Leporello, nervously hiding, now adds his pessimistic comic patter (he told us so) to Anna's cries and the Don's mockery as they struggle.

Anna runs into the house on hearing her father, the old Commendatore, a distinguished figure who now emerges, sword in hand, to challenge the intruder. Their swordplay gleams and flashes briefly in the orchestra but the old man is no match for Don Giovanni. He is soon lying wounded in an extraordinary passage for three bass voices (Leporello is still gibbering in the background) and the orchestra that portrays his life ebbing away.

In hurried recitative the Don reassures his servant (who recovers himself sufficiently to ask whether Donna Anna was in forthcoming mood) and incidentally establishes his callous character, a character apparently incapable of regret. It has been pointed out that Don Giovanni has no memory, no sense of the past; nor has he any fear of the future. Not only is he denied a capacity for responsibility, therefore, but also has to live for the moment; compulsively hurtling from one adventure to the next. He and Leporello hurry off as Donna Anna emerges from the house with her fiancé, Don Ottavio. In a tense accompanied recitative they discover her father's corpse. She is distraught; he is considerate, tender and efficient, ordering help from the servants and having the body quickly removed.

Don Ottavio enjoys the dubious reputation of being the most wimpish tenor in Mozart opera, possibly all opera, a reputation gained chiefly from his rather helpless interjections later on when Anna will recount tonight's events, beginning with attempted rape; but a case could be made for his being an older man, a father figure, as he has been in some recent productions. This would be in keeping with his gentleness and what, despite his lack of martial ardour, seems to be social respectability and organisational efficiency. But most tenors can stand having the character misjudged or despised, since the role has been allocated some of Mozart's most beautiful music to sing.

Donna Anna plunges into their duet with 'Fuggi, crudele, fuggi!' (Leave me, cruel one!) as she rejects her fiancé's attempt to comfort her. Ottavio's tenderness calms her for a moment; the orchestra whirls wonderingly around her as, her head still swimming, she asks for her father. Ottavio answers her, in a falling phrase of loving warmth, that she has both husband and father in him ('Hai sposo e padre in me'). Both end by swearing vengeance on the unknown assailant and the scene closes on a note of brisk determination: the process of retribution has been set in motion.

New prey

Our anti-hero, meanwhile, roams the streets of Seville by night in search of new prey. He scarcely listens as Leporello objects to his life-style. Not only has the Don his eye on another beautiful woman, but he's also distracted, or rather alerted, by the sight of a stranger, a woman in travelling clothes who seems to be looking for someone. The woman is Donna Elvira, and the over-emotional mood we meet her in is typical. Throughout the opera she is usually tearful or angry; and the fact that the Prague première of the opera failed to give her the spectacular solo opportunities allowed Donna Anna (Elvira got an extra aria when the opera was performed in Vienna) led to the role being cast as a *seconda donna*, very much a supporting female role, for most of the nineteenth century – even being considered less important than the soubrette Zerlina who, in the person of such imperious divas as Adelina Patti, would often become the opera's centre of gravity.

This century too saw a tradition of playing her for laughs: poor Donna Elvira, always turning up like a bad penny, a scold and a hysteric, a cross between a schoolmarm and a frustrated spinster. Another dimension perhaps working against her being taken as seriously as she deserves is the occasional class-war interpretation of the Don's victims: if Anna represents the nobility and Zerlina the peasantry, then Elvira must embody that laughable phenomenon, the bourgeoisie.

Her first music ('Ah! chi mi dice mai' – Ah! Who can tell me?) displays those interval leaps which betoken emotional instability in Mozart opera. She muses aloud on the monster who deserted her, adding thoughtfully that she wants to tear out his heart. The eavesdropping men add their sympathetic voices to her in an aside; neither has recognised her yet. Only when the Don swaggers forward to help this damsel in distress does he realise that this is the lady of Burgos whom he seduced and abandoned, even after declaring her his wife. 'She talks like a printed book!' observes Leporello admiringly at her flood of reproachful recitative. The Don says his servant will explain everything and darts away, leaving Leporello to detain this unwelcome figure from the past, which he does with supreme tactlessness.

In an attempt to console her, the servant reads out the list of his master's conquests in the famous Catalogue Aria ('Madamina, il catalogo è questo' – Little lady, this is the catalogue). The tally is formidable: 640 in Italy, 231 in Germany, 100 in France, 91 in Turkey, 'but in Spain already a thousand and three'. Getting into his stride, Leporello enjoys pattering through the types, shapes and sizes that are grist to his master's sexual mill: princesses to peasants, plump, slim, tall or tiny. He ends with the knowing sentiment (matched by a delicately leering musical phrase) that as long as she wears a skirt, we all know what the Don will do. Leporello skips off; the distracted Elvira's recitative in which she declares her intention to seek revenge ends the scene.

A peasant wedding

We move to a group of villagers who are celebrating a peasant wedding. Zerlina and Masetto command their friends to follow their example. She urges the country maidens not to waste time, he exhorts the lads to give up their gallivanting and settle down. The difference in their characters, often overlooked, is subtly emphasised here. Both look forward to the joys of marriage, but Zerlina's amorous eagerness contrasts with her fiancé's level-headed domesticity. The rollicking chorus adds its own bucolic cheerfulness to the merrymaking.

Needless to say, when Don Giovanni and Leporello come across this idyllic scene, the libertine rises to the challenge. He invites the whole party to his mansion, promising entertainment and refreshment, assigning Leporello to go on ahead with them – and to take special care of the bridegroom Masetto. The latter, no fool, objects to being swept off with the rest leaving Zerlina with this stranger; but Don Giovanni's smilingly veiled threats, not to mention the hand moving significantly to his sword, gives the peasant little choice. In an angry little aria ('Ho capito, signor sì' – I've understood, sir), Masetto bitterly obeys his social superior and furiously scolds Zerlina in a mocking refrain.

Leporello bustles him away and the Don and the peasant girl are left alone. From effusively flattering recitative in which he promises to make the dazed girl his bride, the Don launches irresistibly into 'Là ci darem la mano' (There we'll take hands), surely the most beguiling seduction duet in opera. Gentle and caressing, it prompts the bemused Zerlina, after some hesitation, to give in; the two join in a liltingly sensuous refrain in triple time, whose pastoral echo is a more genteel version of the peasants' rustic jollity.

The seducer and his hypnotised victim are moving towards his house when Donna Elvira bursts upon them. She takes the not entirely willing Zerlina under her wing, despite Giovanni's protestations to the peasant girl that she's a poor infatuated creature, and she warns the girl to flee the traitor. 'Ah, fuggi il traditor' is starchy, jagged in rhythm, a schoolmistressly sort of aria, written in an already old-fashioned idiom and deliberately recalling Handel. It ends with a burst of coloratura indignation that corresponds with forefinger-wagging admonition, and Elvira leads Zerlina away.

The Don's exasperation at being balked of his prey is intensified by the appearance of Anna and Ottavio. With relief, he realises that neither recognises him as Anna's attacker. He is professing loyal friendship and enquiring why Anna looks so sad, when who should enter but that irritating recording angel of all his misdeeds, Elvira yet again. She opens the quartet 'Non ti fidar, o misera' (Unhappy woman, do not trust) by warning Anna that the Don is a hypocrite and a liar. The Don tries to laugh it off as the ravings of a lunatic; but Anna and her betrothed are impressed by Elvira's bearing (which goes some way to counter the alternately hysterical/comic image we've received of her through the eyes of the others).

Donna Anna's realisation

The two reflect on the growing doubts they feel about their friend Don Giovanni; Elvira rants; and the Don vacillates between laughing it off and furiously muttering to her to be quiet and avoid a scandal – the threatening undertow to his urgency hints at potential violence. Elvira departs, after promising to shout the Don's perfidy from the rooftops; the Don makes his excuses and follows her in case she does something rash. And like a thunderbolt the orchestra announces Donna Anna's revelation. She has realised who this man is at last.

The great scene begins with the shocked woman's 'Don Ottavio, son morta!' (Don Ottavio, I'm fainting). In accompanied recitative the orchestra adds a note of blazing certainty as she falters out her conviction: that is the man who killed her father. Don Ottavio prompts her, amazed (this is an acid test for the acting abilities of any tenor; Ottavio's comments on his fiancée's story can sound hopelessly, even comically, inadequate), and she recounts the events of that terrible night. A cloaked figure entered her room; at first she took it for Ottavio. When he seized her she screamed; he tried to stifle her cries but she eventually managed to struggle free (the tenor's pious ejaculation of 'ahimè, respiro'– ah me, I breathe again – has been known to prompt guffaws in the audience).

Anna's memories grow more vivid and terrifying as she relives the intruder's flight and her pursuit, her father's intervention and the old man's death. The recitative launches with thrilling impact into her vengeance aria, 'Or sai chi l'onore' (You know now for certain), in which she spurs Ottavio to revenge, its middle section softening as she broken-heartedly recalls her father's wounds and the bloodstained earth. Implacable emotion, hair-raising intensity, tightly controlled music, the aria is considered by many to be the well-spring of the opera.

Left alone, Don Ottavio reflects incredulously on the possibility of Don Giovanni, a nobleman, being capable of such a crime. His slowness to condemn may anticipate the over-

Ruggero Raimondi, a great Don Giovanni on stage, and in Joseph Losey's film, with an all-too-willing victim, in a Covent Garden production.

merciful emperor in *La Clemenza di Tito,* but whereas indulgence is a virtue in rulers, in fiancés of attempted-rape victims it looks uncommonly like spinelessness. He redeems himself musically, however, with 'Dalla sua pace' (On her peace mine depends).

The aria was written for the Vienna production, as the tenor shied away from the challenge to breath-control in 'Il mio tesoro' (Console my beloved) and Mozart produced this substitute aria to be sung earlier in the action. Even given the current purist approach, the opera-goer can feel disappointed if he doesn't get both arias in modern productions. Here Ottavio tenderly affirms that he shares Anna's pleasures and griefs, her tears and sighs. Sheer melting lyricism makes up for any lack of vital characterisation.

We meet the two miscreants, master and manservant, again. Leporello brings the Don up to date in quick, conversational recitative. Leporello has got the peasants drunk and they're happily carousing; even the unexpected arrival of Donna Elvira with Zerlina in tow couldn't faze him. He gently led her into the garden during one of her accustomed rants and has locked her outside in the street. The Don is delighted and bursts into the so-called Champagne Aria (in fact champagne is never mentioned). In 'Fin ch'han dal vino' (As long as there is wine) he orders a feast, with dancing, while the wine makes the guests' heads reel. Any likely girls in the square are to be invited too. He has his own plans: tomorrow the catalogue should be bigger by at least ten . . . . This febrile, slightly mechanical rattling off of directions is the nearest the Don gets to a revealing solo aria.

Alone of Mozart's great operatic protagonists he never confides in us, never gives a glimpse of what makes him tick psychologically. The role is one of opera's greatest challenges not because of any *Hamlet*-like contradictory complexities but because of its pre-eminent blankness: a performer, and producer, can make what they like of the Don, provided it keys in with the other characters' reactions to him.

Zerlina and Masetto

The scene switches to the garden where Zerlina is trying to soothe the sulky Masetto amidst the revelling villagers by insisting that she's done nothing wrong. Zerlina's wheedling sexuality is illustrated by her little aria of pleading, 'Batti, batti' (Beat me, beat me). One recent London production was chastised for making her as sexually aware as the Don, but her music is marked by sensuousness as much as humour or

winsomeness. Here she tells Masetto to beat her, pull her hair, punish her as he will. Seeing Masetto melt, Zerlina ends with a dancing measure in which she invites him to spend days and nights in happiness. Unfortunately for this moment of new-found peace, Zerlina is thrown into agitation at the sound of Don Giovanni's voice off-stage. Masetto mistakes her nervousness for guilt and his suspicions flare up again.

The Act 1 finale opens with Masetto hiding in an alcove to spy on his betrothed and the Don. Zerlina is genuinely frightened, as much for what the Don may do to Masetto as for herself. The nobleman spots her trying to hide among the trees and adopts his most cajoling tone. Following her into the alcove he bumps into Masetto but carries the embarrassment off by pretending concern for the poor lost girl; and invites them indoors to the dancing.

Three masked strangers appear. They are of course Elvira – characteristically taking the lead in a plot to expose the monster – Ottavio and Anna. From inside the palace a minuet can be heard. Leporello and then Don Giovanni look out of the window and invite the strangers to the ball. They accept; and from 'Protegga il giusto cielo' (May heaven protect) ask heaven to protect and avenge them in two lines set with breathtaking beauty that provides an oasis of calm serenity before the storm. The sleekly sensuous sound of their entwining voices combining with the undertow of tugging dramatic urgency provided by the tense situation looks forward to the similar ambiguities of the canon quartet in *Così fan tutte*, and even finds an echo two centuries later in the trio 'Good Frances, do not weep' from Britten's *Gloriana*.

They move into the great hall, brilliantly lit up and whirling with dancers and drinkers. The Don and Leporello ply the guests with refreshments; Zerlina is still nervous, Masetto fuming with jealousy. The host greets the three masked strangers with that cry of '*Viva la libertà*!' that so alarmed the theatre censors of the time. An offstage minuet is heard as everyone resumes dancing. Elvira, possibly enjoying the drama of it all, tells Anna she has spotted Zerlina; the faltering noblewoman has to be encouraged by Ottavio. Now the Don and his servant carry out a two-pronged plan of campaign. The musical texture becomes as complex as the emotional tangles. Anna and Ottavio dance the minuet and the Don chooses Zerlina as his partner in the contredanse, while Leporello drags the protesting Masetto on to the dance floor in a rustic German measure.

When Don Giovanni whisks Zerlina into another room,

Masetto manages to tear himself free of Leporello and make after them. The three avengers break down the door as we hear Zerlina crying for help. She runs out, followed by Don Giovanni brandishing his sword and dragging Leporello whom he claims was the villain of the piece. This cuts no ice with the three avengers; they unmask, and the act ends with the Don threatened with vengeance while he laughingly refuses to show fear.

Given that the stage directions specify a pistol for Don Ottavio at this point, it's hard to know how the Don actually gets away, a problem usually fudged, though bold modern producers offer solutions that range from Douglas Fairbanks athleticism to the metaphysical. It seems more likely that Donna Elvira, volatile, basically warm-hearted and still in love with her seducer, throws herself between the Don and his enemies, allowing him to make an escape, doubtless with a mock-courteous flourish.

Act 2

Certainly the Don is in chipper form at the opening of Act 2. In front of an inn, master and servant are engaging in their usual bout of recriminations and Leporello, complaining about being half-killed in the Don's service, is again on the point of leaving. In the not too serious duet 'Eh via, buffone, non mi seccar' (Now, you clown, don't make me angry) you feel the scene has been acted out countless times already; just as you feel that the Don's placatory offer of four gold pieces was exactly what the servant was angling for.

The men's similar vocal themes remind us of yet another theory about this ambiguous and constantly changing opera: that the Don and Leporello are two sides of the same coin. Certainly there's a tradition of bass-baritones enjoying playing both parts, while the iconoclastic American producer Peter Sellars underlined their closeness by casting twin brothers in the roles; possibly the conjecture that a distinguished performer in both roles shared with me, that the Don might be even more swinging than we thought by having an affair with Leporello, is perhaps carrying modishness too far.

The Don dismisses Leporello's suggestion that he gives up women, explaining that he loves them so much that he must be faithful to them all. It's only because women have no head for figures that they take his good nature for deceitfulness. Tonight he's off to woo Donna Elvira's maidservant, but to quell any suspicions insists on doing it in Leporello's cloak. Elvira herself appears at the window of the inn and in the gathering darkness falls victim to a heartless joke in the trio 'Ah! taci, ingiusto core' (Be silent, unkind heart). As she urges her unfair heart to be still and not to pity the betrayer, the Don stands behind Leporello, now dressed in his master's cloak, and in his most wheedling tone begs her to forgive him. The bittersweet ensemble shows Elvira in loving mood, and now a figure of fun only through the prank played on her, but otherwise with a dignity all her own. Even Leporello comments on the Don's heart of stone. Giovanni briefs Leporello to keep her occupied and out of the way. Elvira hurries out of the inn to meet her love, as she thinks, with pathetic eagerness.

Leporello, keeping his face averted, plays up and is actually beginning to enjoy it when the watching Giovanni cues their departure by creating a disturbance. The unlikely couple hasten away to find privacy; the Don addresses himself to the business of the evening. His serenade 'Deh, vieni alla finestra' (Come to the window), with mandolin accompaniment, is couched in that tone of slightly menacingly romantic charm that characterises the Don. It never achieves its aim, however, since Masetto, armed with pistol and arquebus, enters with a crowd of villagers in search of the seducer. The Don immediately passes himself off as a disgruntled Leporello and sends them in all directions ('Metà di voi qua vadano' – Half of you go that way), leaving Masetto to himself. He eggs the peasant on in his bloodthirsty plans for the Don, and Masetto rashly hands over his weapons for 'Leporello' to admire. This gives the disguised Don the chance to beat Masetto soundly, leaving him knocked flat and bruised black and blue.

That's how Zerlina finds her fiancé when she comes searching by lantern-light. Only another dose of that half-teasing, half-tender sexiness can soothe Masetto's aches and pains, and in an aria ('Vedrai carino' – You shall see, dearest) she promises him her own special cure; a pleasant cure but not one prescribed by any apothecary. She keeps it beating here; and she places Masetto's hand on her breast as she helps him hobble home. Zerlina's sexual identity is as apparent as ever, but here the real tenderness suggests she may have learnt her lesson after her frightening experience with Don Giovanni.

Leporello and Donna Elvira

Meanwhile the uneasy Leporello is by now tiring of the cloying attentions of Donna Elvira, still under the impression that he is a repentant Don Giovanni. He tries to ditch her in a

Luigi Bassi, the creator of the first Don Giovanni in Prague.

dark courtyard. Her tremulous nervousness at being left alone ('Sola, sola, in buio loco' – Alone, alone, in a dark place) begins a sextet. Leporello's is the next voice heard as he blunders and gropes for a doorway in the darkness. He almost collides with Don Ottavio and Donna Anna, both dressed in mourning and still grieving for the Commendatore; Anna's utterances in reply to Ottavio's fond pleas to dry her eyes have a tragic dignity. Their mood contrasts with Leporello's desperation to get away and Elvira's pathetic bewilderment. Suddenly Zerlina and Masetto burst in and grab Leporello whom they take for his master – Donna Elvira's plea for mercy for the man she calls husband has an unconsciously comic ring to it. She alone begs for mercy while the others demand death.

Only when Leporello flings off his master's cloak and falls to his knees does the company realise that it's been tricked once again. Ominous scales in the woodwind accompany his pleas for life; an unexpectedly sombre reminder of the dark mood of the beginning of the overture – could Leporello really be close to death? Anyway, the incorrigible lackey is soon back to comic form, rattling out his patter while the others express shock and bafflement at the latest turn of events – and of course Masetto and Zerlina still assume that he was the one who gave Masetto a beating. In the version of the opera usually performed nowadays, Leporello launches into a gabbled catalogue of excuses, apologies and alibis ('Ah, pietà, signori miei' – Have mercy, gentles all), citing Elvira as his witness, and, getting uncharacteristically flustered, loses the gift of his usually fluent gab and makes a bolt for it.

In the revised version composed for Vienna, Zerlina and Leporello have a scene to themselves where she holds him prisoner, ties him up, threatens him with a razor and, sounding as if she's picked up some of Donna Elvira's vocabulary, compares herself to a tiger, an asp and a lion. The mood of the duet ('Per queste tue manine' – By your little hands, as the whimpering Leporello puts it) is lightened into comedy both by the orchestra and the delight Zerlina expresses in the pleasure of torturing men. Leporello manages to escape with the help of a passing peasant, and when the prototype Miss Whiplash returns with Elvira and Masetto to gloat over the prisoner he has gone.

In the original Prague version, Don Ottavio realises that they have enough evidence against Don Giovanni to denounce him to the authorities. The only question about Don Ottavio's ensuing aria is whom it may be addressed to.

In the ravishing 'Il mio tesoro' (Console my beloved) he orders them – somebody – to comfort his lady, to dry her tears and assure her that he will return, an avenger, with news of death and punishment. Producers have often emptied the stage by now: Donna Anna obviously left some time ago and Masetto and Zerlina ran out after Leporello. Ottavio may be issuing instructions to servants; or he may be addressing the breezes and echoes and attendant spirits of baroque opera. Either way, the aria is a gem, though its runs posed such problems for the tenor that, as we have seen, 'Dalla sua pace' was substituted.

The other Vienna addition, for which we must feel profoundly grateful to Caterina Cavalieri, the new Donna Elvira (and first Constanze in *The Seraglio* six years before), is Elvira's great outburst. The recitative 'In quali eccessi, o numi' (In what enormities, O gods) is accompanied by unexpectedly rich and shifting harmonies as Elvira predicts the wrath of heaven for Don Giovanni, yet admits to conflicting emotions. The aria 'Mi tradì quell'alma ingrata' (That ungrateful soul betrayed me) is a direct outpouring of grief, pity and love which turns Elvira into a romantic heroine. She admits that she feels compassion for the man whose treatment of her deserves punishment; and her heart fails her when she thinks of his danger. Florid, melodic, emotionally charged, this is Elvira's hysterical streak ennobled into the most passionate declaration of feeling in the whole opera; it makes Ottavio look prissy, Don Giovanni mechanical, and the billing and cooing peasants no more profound than cuddly toys.

Donna Elvira may have been referring to the danger from the authorities closing in on Don Giovanni. She may conceivably have had an inkling, some typically emotional intuition, of something darker and more implacable; justice from an even higher court.

We next meet Don Giovanni leaping over a churchyard wall and into a cemetery. He chortles at his evening's pleasures and is soon swapping news with Leporello as they change back into their own clothes. Their bawdy jokes are suddenly interrupted by a mysterious voice that warns Don Giovanni that his laughter will be over by dawn. The Don prowls around the cemetery, striking the statues with his sword until the voice reproves him for disturbing the dead (the distant trombones add an eerie intimation of doomsday).

Still convinced of a practical joke, the Don notices a statue to the dead Comendatore and orders the trembling Leporello to read the inscription. It speaks of awaiting vengeance on his assassin: Leporello is terrified, his master contemptuous. The Don insists on Leporello inviting the statue to supper that night. The duet for the mocking master and his quavering servant ('O statua gentilissima' – O most obliging statue) is a mixture of the sinister and the mundane that explains the opera's popularity among the German Romantics (significantly *Don Giovanni* is the work playing in the opera house next to the tavern in *The Tales of Hoffmann*) and evokes the world of *Struwwelpeter*, where nightmare creatures might dart into everyday surroundings to punish the wicked. The statue nods in acceptance: Leporello is beside himself, his master interested but unafraid. They leave to prepare for their unusual guest.

In a darkened room in Donna Anna's house Don Ottavio is trying to cheer his fiancée into some sort of normality. The knowledge that justice is closing in on Don Giovanni does nothing to assuage her loss; and she shudders at Ottavio's suggestion of an imminent wedding. When he calls her cruel she retaliates. In recitative she explains that it hurts her to postpone their marriage too but they must wait. In the aria 'Non mi dir, bell'idol mio' (Say not that I am cruel), she assures him of her love in broad, serene phrases; but adds that Ottavio must calm his own longing unless he wants her to die of grief.

She puts the wedding off in the vaguest terms – 'perhaps one day heaven will have pity on her'. The coloratura with which she ends the aria hints at hysteria (or perhaps the lady doth protest too much), and it's all too easy to play the psychiatrist and suggest that Donna Anna has either been shocked into frigidity by her experiences or for some reason now finds Ottavio insipid. The loyal Ottavio resolves to stay with her and share her grief, every inch the 'new man'.

The finale

The finale opens with Don Giovanni at his supper table. Some musicians play in the background as he eats – and Leporello tries to escape. The on-stage band plays a medley from current operatic successes: Martín y Soler's *Una cosa rara* (libretto also by Da Ponte), Sarti's *I due litiganti* and Mozart's own *Figaro*, a graceful gesture to the Prague public who had loved the opera so much. Meanwhile Leporello, faint with hunger, snatches the occasional mouthful on the sly, to the amusement of Don Giovanni, who pretends not to notice but teases him by asking him to whistle just when

Leporello's mouth is fully occupied. The light-hearted mood is dispelled in her typical manner by Donna Elvira who comes to beg her faithless lover for the last time to change his way of life. The Don mocks her earnestness (even Leporello is moved) and raises a toast to wine and women.

The resigned Elvira departs; but she returns screaming and rushes out on the other side of the stage. Leporello goes to see what alarmed her. He too rushes back with a yell of fear, slamming the door behind him. The Don can get no sense from his terrified, inarticulate gibbering about the stone statue and its steps going tramp, tramp, tramp . . . . Knocking is heard at the door. The music of the overture returns, like fumes swirling up from the underworld, as Leporello refuses to open the door. He hides under the table as his master himself admits the statue of the Commendatore. He has come to supper. His host courteously orders food to be brought but the jabbering Leporello refuses to budge.

The Commendatore dismisses thought of mortal food; he has a graver purpose – to invite the Don in turn to dine with him. Despite Leporello's statement that his master is otherwise engaged, the Don accepts with bravado, only to cry out at the freezing grip of the statue's hand. The statue urges him to repent (even Leporello, peeping from under the table, thinks it best to join in); the Don defiantly refuses. A ghostly chorus from below and flickering flames herald Don Giovanni's doom and he is dragged, finally shrieking in pain and terror, down to hell. The scene had the power to shock its first audiences; it is still a breath-taking experience, the trombones used like the trump of doom as the Don is summoned to his own judgement day.

The nineteenth century, seeing Don Giovanni as a Byronic free spirit, would end the opera here, a grand, romantic gesture (and comfortingly moral, too, for the more conventionally-minded). The actual final scene is in keeping with our own less emotional age, distancing and detached. Anna, Ottavio, Elvira, Zerlina and Masetto burst in seeking the villain. Leporello stammers out the story; Elvira bears out meeting a spectre; and the characters realise they must put their lives together again.

Don Ottavio, ever hopeful, proposes yet again to Anna; she requests a year for her heart to heal (for her father presumably, though cynics might say Don Giovanni himself was the hardest act to follow) and in twining, elegant phrases they agree to wait. Donna Elvira decides to enter a convent where, one hopes, her temperamental nature will find some calm;

Zerlina and Masetto will go home for dinner; and Leporello is off to the inn to find a new and better master. The six join in a moral sung directly to us, with the slightly cinematic effect of a camera pulling away in long shot . . . . There's an almost detached quality to the words and music: this is the fate of all sinners – evil-doers come to an equally evil end.

'Come, children, let us shut up the box and the puppets, for our play is played out.' The last words of *Vanity Fair* are not entirely inappropriate, for they also ask which of us has his desire; or, having it, is satisfied. Perhaps the secret to Don Giovanni's character is that he never is, can never be, satisfied. Perhaps he has been in hell all along.

A success in Prague, a failure in Vienna. It is said that during an impassioned argument about the new work among opera-goers, someone turned to Haydn for his opinion. He quietly replied, 'I can only say that I consider Mozart the greatest composer alive and *Don Giovanni* the greatest opera I have ever heard.' The Emperor, who in his erratic and capricious way knew Mozart's worth (if not his value), called the opera divine. 'I would say it is even more beautiful than *Figaro*; but it is not a meat suitable for the teeth of my Viennese.' Mozart allegedly retorted: 'Give them time to chew on it.'

The consolation of being appointed to the position of *Kammermusicus*, the royal court composer, in succession to Gluck who had recently died, was slight. The older composer had done relatively little towards the end of his life for a salary of 2,000 gulden. Mozart's pay was 800. The year 1788 saw more letters to fellow-Mason Michael Puchberg begging for loans. The money worries that had harassed Amadé for most of his free-lance life began to assume the nightmare proportions that left him overworked, exhausted and desperate by the time he died three years later. Meanwhile, in heart-rending profusion, the masterpieces continued to pour out.

Chapter 6

Così Fan Tutte

Besides money problems, the summer of 1788 saw the death of the Mozarts' little daughter (only two of the couple's six children survived). With a bittersweet contrast typical of a Mozartian opera, the composer shortly afterwards turned out a string of masterpieces, including the last three symphonies. By 1789 Constanze was pregnant again and her husband indulged in another foray through the courts of Europe. Despite some critical success, especially in enlightened Prussia, whose kings from Frederick the Great onwards had

Prince Karl Lichnowsky (1756-1814), a member of Mozart's Masonic lodge, took the musician to Berlin, via Leipzig and Prague, in the hope of finding work with the King of Prussia.

Constanze Mozart, née Weber, shortly after her marriage.

esteemed music as much as militarism, Mozart returned home with nothing to show for it; and the pitiful letters to Puchberg soon began again.

In August a revival of *Figaro* proved a godsend, for it led to a commission from the Emperor. It is said that Joseph himself suggested the theme of the new work; moreover it has been claimed that the story was based on an actual event – ironically, in view of the fact that the actual, highly improbable, plot of *Così fan tutte* is the most elaborately stylised exercise in rococo artifice among Mozart's operas. In November the Mozarts had another daughter who died at birth. Amadé kept hard at work, not merely on *Così*, scheduled for a January première, but also on the radiant Clarinet Concerto for his friend Anton Stadler.

Mozart and Salieri

By this time it seems that the composer may have been getting paranoid. His letters to the pregnant Constanze while she was taking the cure at Baden had shown unreasonable jealousy and an almost obsessive concern with what other people might say about them. There is a modern tendency to tone down the legendary rivalry between Mozart and Salieri, immortalised for a generation of playgoers and then film fans in *Amadeus*. But it seems certain that Salieri, like many in his position in a professionally – and socially snobbish – competitive world, was indulging in his fair share of backbiting and intriguing. A strange letter exists from Mozart to Michael Puchberg inviting him to attend a rehearsal of the new work, adding 'I am inviting only Haydn and yourself. I shall tell you when we meet about Salieri's plots which have however already completely failed.'

To a certain extent Salieri may have been justified in feeling disgruntled; *Così fan tutte* owed something, as regards plot and libretto, to his own *Grotta di Trofonio*, produced five years earlier. Da Ponte had referred to it throughout its genesis as 'The School for Lovers' – *La scuola degli amanti*; it was Mozart who extracted the words 'così fan tutte' (thus do all women) from the text. It sounds considerably more cynical; or were those fears of conspiracy and betrayal beginning to take their toll?

Characters:
Fiordiligi *soprano*
Dorabella *mezzo-soprano* } two sisters
Despina, their maid *soprano*
Ferrando *tenor*
Guglielmo *baritone* } their fiancés
Don Alfonso a philosopher, *bass*

Act 1

The five syllables of 'così fan tutte' – thus do all women – dominate the opening of the overture. There follows a characteristically bubbling Mozart allegro, scampering along like a charmingly empty-headed bimbo, as fickle and frivolous as the opera's title implies (but things won't be quite what they seem).

The action is set in Naples. The curtain rises on two young army officers carousing with an older man. Their easily sparked hyperbole, and the speed with which they leap at the chance to make a wildly far-fetched bet, suggest that they may have been making a night of it.

Talk has turned to the subject of woman and their faithfulness – or lack of it. In a trio ('La mia Dorabella') Ferrando is praising his fiancée Dorabella, as faithful as she is beautiful.

Guglielmo likewise declares his Fiordiligi incapable of inconstancy. The cynical Don Alfonso, an elderly philosopher, wants to end the argument but the young men insist that he gives some proof of his theories.

The officers challenge him in recitative, with slightly truculent jocularity, to give reasons for his scepticism. He launches a second trio ('È la fede delle femmine' – Woman's faith is like the phoenix) by comparing a woman's fidelity with the phoenix; everyone says it exists but nobody knows where. The young men rapturously declare each of their beloveds to be the phoenix. Don Alfonso snorts that neither the mythic bird nor female faithfulness has ever existed.

The wager

In recitative he turns the tables on his companions by demanding proof of their sweethearts' constancy. He wagers them a hundred sequins that he can show Dorabella and Fiordiligi to be no better than any other mortal woman. Sworn to secrecy, the young men rhapsodise in a trio ('Una bella serenata' – A lovely serenade) how they will spend the money they consider as good as won already. The romantic Ferrando will arrange a serenade to his beloved. Guglielmo, being a baritone, is more down to earth: a banquet will mark his celebration. And will Don Alfonso be invited? asks the philosopher dryly. Of course, and they'll all drink toasts to the god of love. On this convivial note the scene ends. The bet has been made in a spirit of slightly aggressive fun. It will be played out in dead earnest.

The sisters

The scene changes to a garden by the seashore. The sisters Fiordiligi and Dorabella gaze at miniatures of their respective lovers. Their duet is preceded by an exquisitely flowery serenade-like orchestral prelude: the first taste of the fragile sensuousness that characterises the musical tone of Così: a wistful delicacy expressed in vocal lines that are lapped by and embroidered with some of the most beautiful accompaniment of all Mozart's operas. The six-voice work has been called an extended sextet. Perhaps it should be termed a concerto for six voices and orchestra.

At this stage both sisters are similar. Each hymns the charms of her beloved in rhapsodic terms that Lydia Languish in Sheridan's The *Rivals* would recognise. Both add emphasis with florid vocal curlicues and ostentatious vocal interval-leaps before their voices blend in swearing that their love will never change.

Poster advertising the 'new Singspiel' *Così fan Tutte*, or The School for Lovers.

In recitative they reveal themselves as high-spirited, inclined to fun, and basically bored, reduced to reading one another's palms, their interests centred on marriage prospects – a couple of Jane Austen's richer and idler characters rather than her heroines; though, like an Austen heroine, they too are going to find painful self-knowledge.

Their frivolity is dispelled by a plainly shaken Don Alfonso. In an aria of broken, breathless phrases he tries to falter out the shocking news, but has to resort to recitative to get it out. The girls' sweethearts have been ordered off to battle. At this moment they are waiting outside to bid the girls farewell.

The ensuing quintet ('Sento, o Dio' – I feel, O God) is a masterpiece of tongue-in-cheek mixed with real emotion. The two officers tremulously express their grief; more melodramatically, the girls long for death. Both sides are play-acting but only the men know they are doing so. The girls, though sincere, can't resist dramatising the situation, perhaps even enjoying the theatricality of it all. In the face of such heartfelt lamentations the boys can't resist expressing their I-told-you-so satisfaction to Alfonso. His reaction is to tell them to wait and see.

In further hyperbole (recitative), Fiordiligi demands a dagger for herself but is capped by her sister who rather smugly declares that she will die naturally of grief with no need to resort to steel. (A duet for the officers here is usually omitted.)

The lovers depart

The sound of a drum heralds the arrival of the boat that must take the officers away. Soldiers and locals sing a chorus glorifying military life, so conventional as to be almost a send-up of the genre: are they in on the joke as well?

The disturbing emotional ambiguity allied with sensuous beauty that gives Così its unique flavour is crystallised in the quintet 'Di scrivermi' (Write to me every day). All exaggerations swept aside, now that the time to part has come, the girls weep bitterly. In heartbroken, disjointed phrases the lovers pledge to keep in touch – write at least twice a day, begs Dorabella; while Alfonso, almost bursting with laughter, can scarcely keep a straight face.

During a repeat of the chorus Ferrando and Guglielmo embark, the military marches off, and the girls are left incredulously alone with Don Alfonso. In the trio 'Soave sia il vento' (Soft be the wind), one of the score's perfect gems, the women wish their lovers godspeed while even the old cynic stops his chuckling at their heart-touching plea to wind and waves. Relatively austere vocal lines are lapped by the orchestra as gently as the breeze-caressed sea.

I'm not a bad actor, Alfonso admits to the audience after the girls have left, as if to excuse himself for this unmanly display of emotion (or perhaps boasting of the success of his manipulations); and, in case we think he was softening, he adds a few more cynical observations on the subject of women's fickleness.

Despina the maid

The scene changes to a room in the sisters' house. The maid Despina is preparing their chocolate, grumbling at the lot of a servant. A pert soubrette in the *commedia dell'arte* mould, she is not above sampling her mistress' chocolate in a spirit of rebellious egalitarianism. The role has recently been entrusted to mezzo-sopranos, a darker and heavier timbre than the light soprano of tradition, and some producers have even seen Despina as a worldly-wise woman of experience, mature, even middle-aged. This seems to fly in the face of her music, which is sprightly, fleet and mischievous, and a character that reflects less jaded cynicism than light-hearted, adventurous opportunism – and very un-jaded delight in her own ingenuity.

Her down-to-earth ruminations are shattered by the entrance of the sisters in a high state of agitation. Dorabella dramatically takes centre stage: in declamatory recitative she

The Australian baritone John Brownlee as Don Alfonso in the famous pre-war Glyndebourne *Così fan Tutte*.

strikes a tragic pose – one can almost see the trumpeting putti, the sweeping draperies and ornate cartouche on the heroic engraving – before launching into her aria, 'Smanie implacabili' (Implacable furies). The orchestra swirls around her like the agonies that torment her as she longs for death. On hearing her mistresses' news, the maid laughs. As sceptical as Don Alfonso, she assures the sisters that there are many men left. The ladies should entertain themselves – their lovers will be doing so while away. Despina's aria 'In uomini, in soldati' (Hope for faithfulness in men?) mocks the idea of male fidelity. She advises the women to pay men back in their own kind.

Strangers arrive

The equally hard-bitten Don Alfonso enlists the maid's help in his conspiracy. He bribes her to support his efforts to console the two ladies with some amorous diversion. Without divulging the identity of the new suitors, he introduces Ferrando and Guglielmo, exotically disguised as Albanians.

The sextet 'Alla bella Despinetta' (To dearest little Despina) begins with Alfonso's presentation of the elaborately moustachioed figures to the maid. It works: Despina is hilariously intrigued but fails to recognise her mistresses' fiancés. The men breathe a sigh of relief – so far so good – while Despina giggles at the outlandish strangers.

Dorabella and Fiordiligi sweep on, annoyed at this unwanted intrusion into their mourning. They too are taken in but not amused; and outraged by the strangers' immediate protestations of devotion (in asides Alfonso and Despina think, as we do, that the ladies protest too much).

Alfonso, who has been lurking discreetly in the background, comes forward with feigned joy and amazement. He greets the Albanians as old friends. The latter promptly lay siege to the sisters. Dorabella wonders what to do (perhaps already interested?) but Fiordiligi repels them in a showpiece aria. 'Come scoglio'(Like a rock) is fiendishly difficult to sing, with its leaps over yawning vocal chasms. Mozart may have taken a certain malicious pleasure in composing it for a soprano who demanded the chance for ostentatious technical virtuosity, but – as with the Queen of the Night's dazzling coloratura in *Die Zauberflöte* – he keeps it carefully in character. Fiordiligi's heroic posturings, comparing herself to a rock resisting gale and tempest and ending with indignant roulades of florid defiance, are certainly over the top; but the tongue-in-cheek comment is Mozart's, gently observing ridiculous extremes of style while never doubting the sincerity of the content.

About to sweep out, the sisters are delayed sufficiently for Guglielmo's aria ('Non siate ritrose' – Don't be shy): nothing too high-flown and almost laughing at itself, the little song catalogues the men's charms, ending with those plumes of love, their whiskers.

This time the two girls do make a scandalised exit. In a rollicking trio ('E voi ridete?' – And you're laughing?) the two suitors explode in laughter while Alfonso tries to quieten them. In recitative he reminds them the wager's time-span lasts until the following morning. In reply to Guglielmo's plaintive query about food, Ferrando muses how a breath of love ('Un'aura amorosa') is sustenance enough. The aria is exquisitely courtly, with an elegance and grace that characterise the idealistic Ferrando and lift him above the mundane rompings of his fellow-plotters.

Alfonso and Despina confirm their partnership in recitative and resolve to redouble the attack on the ladies' virtue. The scene changes to a garden. In swooningly beautiful music the sisters reflect on the extraordinary day. The introspective quality of the music gives way to the dramatic exclamations of the men who rush on with phials and, despite Alfonso's attempts to stop them, apparently drain the poison therein. The suitors collapse; the ladies helplessly call Despina who hurries away with Alfonso to find a doctor; and the two couples are left together.

Noting their swains are still breathing, the girls draw nearer – after all, as Fiordiligi observes, one can't abandon them like this. More to the point, Dorabella remarks how interesting their faces are. The sisters feel the men's foreheads and pulses, evidently moved.

Alfonso returns with a doctor – in fact Despina in disguise, as seen at once by the men though not by her distraught mistresses. In best *commedia* tradition, she rattles off mock-erudition before producing a magnet – 'mesmeric stone', a reference to Dr Mesmer – and galvanises the poison victims into life (quivering trills from the orchestra). The girls hold the men's heads to control their convulsions but are taken aback when the dazed patients refer to them as Pallas and Venus. They insist on a kiss (explained by Alfonso and Despina as the potion's after-effects) but, after a moment's hesitation, the women rally and furiously flounce out, leaving the rest of the company in helpless laughter.

Act 2

Next morning Despina needles her edgy mistresses and persuades them at least to let the strangers return – and then play it by ear. In an aria ('Una donna a quindici anni') she voices her philosophy: that a girl of fifteen knows what's what; and that a woman should get her own way.

The sisters profess shock at her attitude, but perhaps rather mechanically. Surprisingly, it's the stronger-willed Fiordiligi who first wonders whether they should heed her advice.

Dorabella seizes the chance to point out how harmless it would be: and suddenly they are duetting over how to allot the young men ('Prenderò quel brunettino' – I will take the dark one) Dorabella opts for the dark, witty one (Guglielmo) while her sister anticipates amusing talk with the fair one (Ferrando). Their voices entwine excitedly at the prospect of entertainment after recent shocks, and they are soon fantasising about the flirtation in store.

In the garden by the seashore the young men mount their final assault, from a garlanded barge, with singers and musicians. Beautifully sedate yet languorously sensuous, their duet with chorus sums up the paradox of *Così*: an artificial plot and a cynical message allied to some of the loveliest music Mozart ever composed.

The girls are understandably dumbstruck; so, almost, are their suitors, now playing shy. Don Alfonso impatiently prompts the men in a quartet, while Despina acts out the women's response, first a dignified reference to the past, then gracious surrender. She and Alfonso add a *sotto voce* patter aside in the best comic opera manner as they take their leave, gleefully convinced that the sisters are ripe to fall.

Seduction

After some bashful small talk about the weather and the garden, Ferrando and Fiordiligi stroll off, leaving the coast clear for Guglielmo to woo Dorabella. In a melting duet ('Il core vi dono' – the heart I give you) she finally yields: with tender urgency Guglielmo removes her locket-portrait of Ferrando and replaces it with a heart-shaped pendant – above her own heart that beats as his. Half-joking, half-loving, nervous, delicately exploring, the duet is as convincing a seduction scene as any in *Don Giovanni*.

They move off as the other pair return. Fiordiligi shows her mettle by rejecting Ferrando's passionate advances (Ferrando's aria here, 'Ah, lo veggio' – Ah, I see it – is often omitted). Alone Fiordiligi reveals her true depths. The reverse side of her granite-willed Act 1 aria is the vulnerable, guilty girl drawn to the stranger and anguished at her own inconstancy. A long recitative expresses her pain. The introspective *rondo* with a lovely horn obbligato, 'Per pietà' (For pity's sake), shows her vacillating between new love and remorse. She finally resolves to be steadfast to her absent love.

Soul-searching

The men meet and compare notes. Ferrando is jubilant: his

friend's fiancée is purity itself. Guglielmo becomes bitter as he realises how he must hurt his friend with a less favourable report on Dorabella. Ferrando is shattered. His first impulse is to kill his faithless sweetheart. Guglielmo calms him with the cynical philosophy of his aria 'Donne mie, la fate a tanti' – Women, you do it to so many. He adores women but their behaviour is not worth defending. Their lovers are right to complain. The sentiments recall Figaro's climactic outburst, but Guglielmo is naturally neither heartbroken nor humiliated. His music amounts to a cheerfully sardonic shrug.

Ferrando's grief, however, puts him on a par with the serious Fiordiligi and her soul-searching. For the first time we appreciate the irony of how mismatched the original couples were. In a cavatina 'Tradito, schernito' (Betrayed, mocked), his hurt and anger give way to the admission that he still loves the fickle Dorabella. Alfonso urges the men to wait. The bet expires tomorrow (this is less a sympathetic hope that things may turn out well after all than the desire to win both parts of the wager instead of merely half).

A parallel scene takes place amongst the women: cynical Despina, changeable Dorabella and unhappy Fiordiligi – who at last confesses her guilty love for the stranger. Dorabella, like Guglielmo, gives vent to cheerful pragmatism. In the skittish 'L'amore è un ladroncello' (Love's a little thief) she surrenders to Cupid, who after all can never be resisted.

By herself Fiordiligi regrets confiding in the others. She decides to disguise herself as a soldier and follow her absent lover to the war; another grand, romantic and faintly ridiculous gesture. Has even the scrupulous Fiordiligi yet to grow up? Guglielmo, eavesdropping in the next room, is proud of her (and himself). This goads Ferrando into action. In the duet 'Fra gli amplessi' (In the embraces) he breaks in on Fiordiligi's preparations to leave and threatens suicide. She finally admits love and their voices blend in a rapturous duet that suggests that Mozart believes them genuinely in love, ideally suited all along – though perhaps Ferrando doesn't realise it.

This time Guglielmo is furious. Don Alfonso, happy that he has after all won his bet, tries to console them. He can see both men still love their fiancées. They should make the best of a bad job; nobody's perfect; the ideal mate never existed. He looks forward to a double wedding – but not before things are tangled a little more for some final fun before all is unravelled. In 'Tutti accusan le donne' (Everyone accuses women) he declares that it's women's nature to be fickle. The

The Dresden Court Theatre, one of many institutions that remembered Mozart with concerts and benefits remarkably soon after his death.

man has only himself to blame. Nothing personal but 'così fan tutte' – all woman are the same. The two suitors join their voices to his in this resounding moral conclusion, to the strains of the phrase we remember from the overture.

Things move swiftly to a climax. Despina and Alfonso supervise the wedding preparations in bustling music addressed to servants and musicians. The chorus greets the two happy couples whose billing and cooing leads to a toast and a ravishing canon quartet in which voices twine sensuously and only Guglielmo reminds us of the men's pain by muttering longingly of poison.

The lovers return

Don Alfonso announces the notary. It turns out to be Despina in disguise again, this time as a dryly pedantic old lawyer who draws out the legalities to an unconscionable length, much to the impatience of the betrothed. Only the women have time to sign the marriage contract before the sound of drums is heard outside, followed by a familiar martial chorus. Don Alfonso rushes to the window and returns shocked: the girls' former lovers are back, disembarking at this very moment.

Panic ensues. The wedding feast and its trappings are rapidly dismantled as the bridegrooms are bundled out to hide. As the women wring their hands in terror, Don Alfonso assures them all will be well. He has his reasons.

Ferrando and Guglielmo come in as themselves, in the military uniforms they wore when they departed. They sing exultantly (and, we know, ironically) of being restored to the arms of their loyal sweethearts. Alfonso feigns amazed joy; only the girls seem speechless. Guglielmo spots a man in hiding – a lawyer, alias Despina, who promptly explains that she has just come back from a fancy-dress ball. Even the men admire her quick wits while the girls, also aside, are genuinely amazed at the notary's identity. Ferrando picks up the marriage contract and both men act out jealous fury. Their remorseful fiancées admit their sin, beg for death, and look to Don Alfonso to explain everything. The men storm into the room where the Albanians were hiding and re-emerge with the latter's clothes.

In music that recalls the mock wooing and Despina's medicinal magnetics, Ferrando and Guglielmo reveal the truth. Don Alfonso, as ever, lowers the temperature and calms hot tempers by exhorting them to embrace and laugh, 'as I have and shall again'. A short ensemble of loving, penitent relief from the ladies, forgiveness from the men and total comic bewilderment from Despina – the sharp-witted schemer outwitted and manipulated all along the line – leads into a contented final chorus singing the virtues of reason and moderation. What others weep at will give you cause for mirth: the only way to find sweet calm in this stormy world.

Ambiguities

So ends the most ambiguous of Mozart's operas. Do we believe in the happy ending? By naturalistic standards (applied to the emotions depicted, not the plot's patently absurd details), nothing can ever be the same again between the former sweethearts. Fiordiligi for one seems to have fallen sincerely in love with the wrong man. The tendency of modern productions is to underline the bitter in the bittersweet mixture. In David Freeman's famous production for Opera Factory the characters sing the final chorus in misery, the men ashamed, the women on the verge of nervous breakdowns. English National Opera's recent version, set in the 1950s, gives the last word to women and budding feminism: the sisters pack their bags and march off. Most producers take Mozart's heartfelt love music at face value and show the 'wrong' couples falling in love, thus making the final reconciliation either scathingly cynical or agonisingly tragic.

And yet . . . the final chorus is in praise not of love, not sentiment, but reason. The two betrothed couples have undergone ordeals as real as those as fairy-tale tests of fire and water in *The Magic Flute*; ordeals described in terms of sensibility and feelings (much as an Austen heroine attains maturity), calculated to purge the women of their high-flown, flowery romanticism, and the men of their exaggerated concept of honour and almost inhuman – certainly unreasonable – constancy. Reason and moderation emerge as the lasting virtues, all the more for the deliberately artificial plot of intrigue, depicting the frailty of human nature when subjected to intolerable – and, be it remembered, unnaturally engineered – pressure.

Far from being a tragedy, as some critics see it today, or a heartless exercise in frivolity, as it was once thought, *Così* is a wise and humane comedy that warns us not to probe our feelings too deeply precisely because it acknowledges their power and danger. It conducts us, like Orpheus, to those depths only so that we can appreciate the sunny uplands all the more. At any rate its layers of love, pain, comedy, disillusion and forgiveness are clothed in music perfect for its function: to escort the characters on a journey to self-knowledge.

The new opera had its première at the Burgtheater on January 26 1790. It was a success. It also proved a swansong for the Mozart-Da Ponte partnership and for the Emperor who had suggested it. Within a month Joseph II was dead, still in his forties. In a slightly disorganised and haphazard way he had abolished serfdom in his vast central European empire, reformed the tax system and curtailed the power of the nobles. Above all, as far as posterity is concerned, he had been the sometimes cranky, but loyal, supporter of Mozart. The new emperor, his brother, had different priorities.

Chapter 7

The Quest Begins:
The Magic Flute (1)

Leopold II, the new Holy Roman Emperor, was as much a reformer as his brother but considerably more efficient as an administrator. His grand duchy of Tuscany had been well governed and once he acceded to the imperial throne he turned his attention to Austria's relationships with a troubled Europe, whose nations were, in 1790, nervously eyeing revolutionary France and wondering whether the contagion would spread.

He dismissed the reputedly unsavoury adventurer, Lorenzo Da Ponte, early on and the Italian deemed it expedient to leave Vienna quickly. Leopold seems to have shown little interest in Herr Mozart's requests for the position, if not of court Kapellmeister (the Emperor confirmed Salieri in that position), then of second Kapellmeister. Given Amadé's by now neurotic conviction that Salieri was conspiring against him, the Emperor's first visit to the opera since his succession, to Salieri's *Axur, Re d'Ormus*, must have been particularly hard to bear.

The composer's begging letters to his patient friend Michael Puchberg continued unabated. The summer was marked by ill health, both Constanze's and his own, with signs that Mozart was suffering from a kidney disease that had struck him before. He fell back on teaching, that old if unloved standby for making ends meet, and among his pupils was Franz Xaver Süssmayr, who would complete the Requiem left unfinished at Mozart's death.

A trip to Frankfurt

In the September of an increasingly desperate year Mozart suffered a snub when the King of Naples, in Vienna for a double royal wedding, was entertained with operas by Salieri and Josef Weigl as well as a gala concert; but Mozart was not asked to contribute. He decided to pawn his silver, hire a car-

Emanuel Schikaneder: writer, comic, actor, singer, impresario and co-creator of *The Magic Flute*.

riage, and go to Frankfurt, where Leopold was to be crowned Emperor of the Holy Roman Empire.

Mozart set off in the unpredictable high spirits that in retrospect cast him in an almost manic-depressive mould. His letters about the journey recall his youthful optimism (at Regensburg he 'ate as well as the English and drank a superb Moselle wine'). As far as work was concerned Frankfurt proved a disappointment, though Mozart played at least two of his piano concertos. By a nice irony of fate, as he reported sardonically to Constanze, on his way back to Vienna he stopped at Munich where the Elector Karl Theodore invited him to perform in a concert for the King and Queen of Naples – from whose celebrations Mozart had been excluded in Vienna.

He returned home in November to find an invitation to London from an English impresario: a six-month stay and two operas were stipulated. Mozart also met the entrepreneur Salomon who was persuading Haydn to come to England with him. The older man, getting on for sixty, accepted – and would make a fortune. Amadé refused all offers; he was tied to Vienna, convinced that something would turn up. Meanwhile he taught and composed (brilliantly, as his last piano concerto attests).

The requiem mystery

By March 1791 the impresario-actor-singer-writer Emanuel Schikaneder, a fellow-Mason, had presented Mozart with the first instalments of a libretto for a German opera. The composer threw himself into this work, staying in Vienna when Constanze made one of her now customary journeys to Baden. As spring ripened into summer, exhaustion set in. In July a sixth child was born (Franz Xavier Wolfgang, who survived), and it was at about this time that Mozart received a mysterious commission for a requiem mass from an unnamed patron. This much-romanticised episode is easily explained. A dilettante, Count Franz von Walsegg, wanted to commission a mass for his late wife that he could pass off as his own. The tired and ailing Mozart superstitiously accepted the commission. He had also received a request from the estates of Bohemia for an opera to celebrate the Emperor's coronation in Prague, but it was the requiem that came to obsess him, as it would even on his deathbed.

Of the three main works that now absorbed Amadé's energies – the official assignment for the state occasion, the mysteriously requested requiem, and the German comic-romantic piece with its unashamed populist show-biz priorities – it would be the last-named, composed for a little suburban theatre, that would be the greatest success, and its popularity would cast a glow over Mozart's last grim days.

Freemasonry

Emanuel Schikaneder was a seasoned writer and actor, specialising in the broad comedy of Hanswurst (Jack Sausage), a traditional German clown figure (though he had played Hamlet in his twenties). He was also a committed Freemason. Although Scottish masons claim earlier records, the first masonic lodge in its accepted modern sense was the Grand Lodge of England in 1717; others followed in Ireland and Scotland, then America, the British colonies and Europe. The future Emperor Francis I had introduced Freemasonry into Germany, ironically in view of his marriage to the reactionary Maria Theresa.

When he was eleven years old Mozart had set a masonic text to music to thank a doctor who tended him during a smallpox epidemic. Dr Mesmer, Mozart's patron Baron Swieten, and others concerned with music, letters, the arts and sciences influenced Mozart to take the steps that led to his initiation in 1784; both his father and Haydn would follow his example. Masonry provided a meeting-point for those with liberal views interested in the problems for which neither church nor state seemed to offer any answer. Given the present-day criticism of the secrecy that still attends the workings of masonry, and the suspicion that it makes up a self-promoting group of powerful allies in business, law and politics, it is as well to remember how progressive, radical and forward-looking the movement was in the eighteenth century, when rationalism clashed with the old certainties of organised religion.

By the 1780s the Craft had fallen into official disfavour in Vienna, and *The Magic Flute* with its references and ritual may well have been intended as a piece of propaganda for masonry. It was garnished with low comedy, romantic and thrilling adventure and scenic effects; Schikaneder was after all a man of the theatre. Musically, too, it remains a wonderful mixture, with its echoes of folksy, popular German song, its near-religious solemnity, and the emotional music given to real people experiencing real feelings.

One wonders how much of this inspired kaleidoscope was accidental, or at least arrived at more by luck than judgement. We know that there were hiccups during the writing of the libretto (and today newcomers may be puzzled by the switch from good-to-bad and bad-to-good of the Queen of the Night and her ladies on one hand and Sarastro on the other; and what about the three boys, commended by the forces of evil, but who turn out to be good?). But, paradoxically, it may be this very mixture that guarantees the work's survival. It says something to every age – and every age-group.

There was a summer-house near Schikaneder's theatre. Here Mozart composed and he could also relax with members of the theatre company. His social life seems to have been as full as his work-load. A feverish round of sociability and composition made up days that would end at 2AM and begin again after a couple of hours' sleep. Mozart appears to have been terrified of loneliness, especially when his wife was away. The theatre, coffee-houses and taverns were scoured in search of friends or someone to talk to. He wrote to Constanze complaining of a dreadful emptiness inside him.

By August his wife was back and was able to accompany Amadé on the trip to Prague for the première of his coronation opera. In normal circumstances this would have been a wonderful opportunity for the composer to lavish that vital gift for humanising conventional characters and formal situations on yet another stilted *opera seria* – and to catch the eye of possible imperial patrons. This time, the overworked and hard-driven Mozart almost regarded the trip to his beloved Prague as an interruption in the real business of the time, the composition of *The Magic Flute*. Only a fortnight after the première of *La Clemenza di Tito* in Prague the *Flute* would be playing in the Vienna suburbs; and three months after that Mozart would be dead, at the age of thirty-five.

Chapter 8

Imperial Interlude:
La Clemenza di Tito

As the carriage bowled towards the Bohemian capital, Mozart was still working on this opera celebrating imperial mercy and munificence, possibly with a certain scepticism. Not only had the new emperor shown himself less interested in Amadé's music than his late brother had been, but the commission of the opera itself had triggered a mortifying contretemps that did no good to the harassed composer's self-esteem.

To begin with, the request for a celebratory work for Leopold's coronation in his Bohemian kingdom had originally been directed to Salieri by the Bohemian Estates. The Italian was busy, so the authorities gladly approached Mozart, whose music had always been so loved in Prague. The Viennese authorities reacted emphatically against this. Their vehemence obviously took the Bohemians by surprise and remains inexplicable today; perhaps one can detect the fine Italian hand of a scheming Salieri behind the fuss. At any rate, the ancestors of the Czech 'velvet revolution' could stick their heels in even then, and they held out for Mozart. To avoid unseemly scandal over a matter involving state pomp and the highest personages in the land, the Viennese gave in; but the affair must have left a nasty flavour and helped convince Amadé that the *Flute* was more worthy of his attention from every point of view.

Mozart was helped with *Tito* by his pupil Franz Xaver Süssmayr, now his loyal amanuensis, today best known for completing his teacher's Requiem but himself the eventual composer of nearly thirty *singspiels* and comic operas. He probably wrote most of the *secco* recitative in the opera. Another friend present was Anton Stadler, for whom Mozart composed parts for basset-horn and clarinet in two arias (and for whom he would find time to write the lovely Clarinet Concerto when they returned to Vienna).

The libretto by Caterino Tommaso Mazzolà was based on another, nearly sixty years old, by the prolific Pietro Metastasio. The libretto was shortened and fine-tuned, and the distinguished designer Pietro Travaglia was brought out of retirement to advise on the sets.

The first performance took place on September 6 1791, in the evening of the coronation day, and was not the last coronation commission to fall flat. Benjamin Britten's *Gloriana* was considered equally unedifying for a celebratory occasion in 1953; but no British royalty would arrive an hour late; nor did they show the crassness and arrogance of the Italian-born Empress who referred to *La clemenza di Tito* as 'porcheria tedesca' – 'German filth'. She, unlike posterity, evidently preferred Salieri.

Characters:
The Emperor Titus (Tito) *tenor*
Sextus (Sesto) *mezzo-soprano*
Annius (Annio) *mezzo-soprano*
Vitellia *soprano*
Servilia *soprano*
Publius (Publio), *bass*

The overture is as stately as expected in a ceremonial opera about the preoccupations of the great, while melodic warmth and instrumental colour remind us that the story also concerns love and friendship. It further reminds us that the composer had masterpieces of psychological character-painting to his credit and was able to inflect even the stilted attitudinising of old *opera seria* with humanity.

Act 1

The apartments of Vitellia, the daughter of the deposed Roman emperor. The rancorous princess, resentful at being passed over as a bride for the new emperor Tito (Titus), is persuading Sesto (Sextus) to join in a conspiracy against him. The opera's opening duet contrasts meltingly affectionate phrases ('Come ti piace' – Whatever you will) as the infatuated young patrician assures Vitellia that he will do anything she desires with the plotting woman's calculation – in the orchestra the strings flicker beneath her carefully controlled vocal line with those leaping intervals that hint at her volatility. Sesto's tender request for a kind glance emphasises the difference between their personalities. It is a brief duet, but already we understand their very different motives.

Pietro Metastasio, whose stately, monumental libretti for *opera seria* are chiefly remembered for the theme that inspired Mozart's *La Clemenza di Tito*, nearly a decade after the poet's death.

Sesto's friend Annio (Annius) brings the news that the Emperor has dismissed Berenice, the Jewish princess whom he was expected to marry. Vitellia undergoes the first of her many rapid changes of mood in the opera and puts the conspiracy on hold, to the distress of the devoted but bewildered Sesto. She calms him in a rather perfunctory manner with an aria ('Deh, se piacer mi vuoi' – If you want to please me) in which her calculating character reveals itself a little more. Her pious references to trust and her condemnation of suspicion evoke the interval-leaping of Fiordiligi's vocal line in 'Come scoglio' – and we know what became of those protestations of fidelity. Vitellia's final reassuring platitudes to her pining admirer trip out almost too pat.

After she leaves, Annio and Sesto affirm their friendship, soon to be cemented in the marriage between Annio and Sesto's sister Servilia. Their duet of tender friendship ('Deh, prendi un dolce amplesso' – With a sweet embrace) has an almost pastoral feel to it. Again the contradictions of the opera are underlined: that Mozart was obviously happier composing the warmly intimate music of human relationships than cladding the statuesque face of public ceremonial with pomp.

That he remembered the state function of *Clemenza*, however, is illustrated by the rich symphonic orchestral writing of the march that introduces us to the Roman Forum. The Roman populace hails Tito who, in a long passage of conversational recitative, informs Sesto that their families are to be united: the Emperor wishes to marry Servilia. Both Sesto and his friend are dismayed, but Annio puts a brave face on it for Sesto's sake; and both young men profess approval of the Emperor's choice. In an aria ('Al più soglio' – Of the supreme office) Tito reflects that the happiness of rewarding merit and benefiting his friends makes the responsibilities of empire worthwhile, otherwise all would be torment and drudgery. Again the music's tone is warmly lyrical.

Servilia enters, only to receive the news of the Emperor's unexpected favour from the lips of her beloved Annius. In a ravishing duet ('Ah, perdona al primo affetto' – Forgive the early love) of simple, affectionate sweetness, the couple can do little but affirm their devotion to each other.

In the grounds of the imperial palace Publio (Publius), captain of the Praetorian Guard, hands the Emperor a list of plotters against him. Tito is more pitying than angry and decides to forgive them. The nobility of his character is borne out by his reaction to Servilia's confession that she loves Annio. In 'Ah, se fosse intorno al trono' (If only there were around the throne) Tito praises her honesty. The quick pulse of generosity beats in his music as he leaves her with the hope that she may be free to marry her love after all.

Vitellia enters to offer her congratulations to the Emperor's betrothed. She mistakes Servilia's encouragement to hope on her own account for mockery and flies into a characteristic rage. When Sesto unwisely shows his face she urges him to put their plot into action. The Capitol must be set on fire and Tito killed. She goads him by revealing that she loves Tito and that as long as the Emperor lives Sesto has a rival. No wonder the emotionally battered Sesto yields with a cry of 'Fermati, io cedo!' (Stop! I give in). Vitellia impatiently demands to know what he's waiting for.

Their scene of recitative ends with Sesto's great aria 'Parto, parto' (I go, I go). The stately formality of its opening expresses his sudden decisiveness; but the music soon softens into praise of Vitellia's beauty. Here Mozart wrote a clarinet obbligato for his friend Anton Stadler, who accompanied him to Prague to play in the first performance. The climactic florid passages in the vocal writing alternate with elaborate

MOZART.

Engraved for the Encyclopædia Londinensis 1819.

instrumental runs, making the aria a showpiece for both singer and player.

His courage screwed to the sticking point, Sesto hurries off to carry out Vitellia's orders. But the situation is dramatically altered by Publio and Annio bringing the news that the Emperor has now chosen Vitellia as his consort.

To churning orchestral turbulence, Vitellia launches a trio in which her agitation at the conspiracy she has set in motion contrasts with the two men's well-meaning comments on how joy can throw a heart into confusion. Their bland vocal parts are topped and embroidered by Vitellia's vocal line, agile and typically wide-ranging.

A quick scene-change to the Capitol, and Sesto muses, in a mixture of terror and determination, on the crime he has to commit. In powerful accompanied recitative he realises he is a traitor to the world's worthiest ruler, a friend to whom he owes everything. He has just decided to defy Vitellia's spite and abandon the plot when he sees the Capitol burning in the distance. The soliloquy with its alternating moods of courage, fear and guilt ending with remorse breathes life into the stilted old tradition of *opera seria* posturing. After the long recitative Sesto launches into 'Deh, conservate o dei' (Oh gods, protect), in which he prays for Tito to be spared or his own life to end. He rushes off to salvage what he can from the situation.

The tension is maintained as Annio and then Servilia run in. The horrified crowd is heard outside and Publio announces that there is a conspiracy afoot. While they wonder who could be responsible for such treachery, Vitellia, by now frightened and remorseful, and the returning Sesto, announcing Tito's death with an anguished vocal line, add their voices to the ensemble. Vitellia urges the hysterical Sesto to keep quiet; and the act ends with principals and chorus in a sombre, restrained lament.

For all its static quality, the libretto has here provided Mozart with the opportunity for one of those stretches of music – high drama, new characters entering, the plot taking new twists – that showed his gift for theatrical action and psychological development. Given the restrained conventions of the already out-dated style of *opera seria*, the Act 1 finale is extraordinarily flexible and shot through with dramatic urgency. Not all of *Tito* keeps the level so high.

Act 2

Act 2 opens with Sesto confessing his guilt to Annio and deciding to flee into exile; Annio explains that Tito has sur-

Josefa Duschek. Married to a composer and a famous singer in her own right, Josefa was a close friend (and, some have conjectured, something more) of Mozart, who wrote concert arias for her.

vived and his aria 'Torna di Tito al lato' (Return to Tito's side) is a generalised aria of pleading or advice. He urges his friend to make a clean breast of it and throw himself on the Emperor's mercy. The music has touching charm but not much individual character or personality.

After Annio's exit Sesto is accosted by Vitellia who begs him to fly – to save his life and her reputation (Vitellia's first concern, as ever, is herself). Sesto protests he would never implicate her, but she shrewdly observes that it is not Tito's severity that is the danger but his kindness. That indulgence may well be Sesto's undoing – she obviously knows her pliable man. Their conversation is interrupted by Publio. He has come to arrest Sesto, who was seen stabbing an imperially-robed figure. It was not the Emperor, however, but another plotter, Lentulus.

There follows a passage dominated by Sesto's exquisite farewell to Vitellia ('Ingrata, addio!' – Ungrateful one, farewell) where he tells her that the breeze playing around her will be his dying sighs. Beautiful woodwind writing and limpid melodic line are more intimately lyrical than tragic; the mood is almost that of a serenade. The pace quickens as Sesto assures Vitellia that he adores her; she expresses grief and fear; and Publio urges his prisoner to accompany him, while admitting the pity he feels. Formal and conventional, the passage makes one regret the speed of the opera's composition. Mozart might have created a heart-rending trio from the situation in different circumstances.

The scene changes to an audience hall in the palace, thronged with patricians, populace and Praetorian Guard. Again the music is surprisingly delicate, as if Mozart was trying to reduce these stiff, neo-classical figures from epic to human scale. The chorus gives thanks for Tito's escape from assassination in music so beautiful and introspective that it belongs more to a stroll along the seashore in *Così fan tutte* than to the public face of state occasions.

In dialogue with Publio, the Emperor expresses his faith in Sesto, who is even now being tried by the Senate. The more sceptical Publio responds with a moralising passage about those who are most honest and loyal being unable to imagine disloyalty in others. The gracefully flowing orchestral accompaniment performs a humanising function on what might easily be a set of platitudes.

Alone, Tito muses on Sesto's friendship and the affection between them. Surely nothing could have changed that. But Annio and Publio return from the Senate with bad news. Sesto has confessed his guilt. The Senate has condemned him and his accomplices to be thrown to the wild beasts in the arena. Annio pleads for mercy on behalf of his friend. In 'Tu fosti tradito' (You were betrayed) he admits Sesto deserves death but begs the Emperor to listen to his heart. The music begins as declamatory and formal, but melodic warmth and agile vocal writing reveal the human being under the classical stance.

Tito's ensuing soliloquy starting with the dramatic recitative 'Che orror! che tradimento!' (What horror! What treason!) at last gives the Emperor the chance to appear something more than an impossibly benign goody-goody. He actually rages against the false friend whose apparent affection concealed a murderous plot. He takes the pen to sign Sesto's death warrant but hesitates, unable to condemn his friend without a personal hearing. He goes on to muse, in the time-honoured way of stage monarchy, how the humble peasant in his rustic hut sleeps sweetly and passes carefree days, unlike a ruler who can trust no man.

The martial mood of the orchestra underlines Tito's new-found sternness as Sesto is brought in. The passage develops into a trio as Tito and Publio comment on the traitor's fear and Sesto trembles in anguish. The climax – with an unexpect-edly quiet conclusion – marks a vintage Mozartian ensemble, though gentler and (again the word is unavoidable) more intimate than we might expect from the libretto's large-scale heroic attitudes.

When they are left alone, Tito admits he wants to pardon Sesto; he exhorts his old friend to explain what drove him to treason. He repeatedly asks for Sesto's confidence, but the young noble refuses to reveal anything beyond his own responsibility, taking all the blame on himself. When he finally asks for death, the Emperor's patience snaps and he calls the guard to take the prisoner away. Sesto, of course, breaks into a farewell aria ('Deh, per questo istante solo' – Pray, for this single moment) of melting affection in which he begs Tito to remember their friendship. In a resolute middle section he faces death without fear, but tormented by the thought of his disloyalty to Tito.

Sesto is led off, his fate sealed. The Emperor muses on the hard heart required by sovereigns, and in floridly agile music asks the gods to change his heart or his sovereignty. In a broodingly pensive middle section he affirms that he wants to win his subjects' loyalty through love not fear.

Servilia and Annio encounter Vitellia. They beg her to intercede for Sesto: the Emperor will refuse her nothing since he has decided to celebrate their marriage forthwith. Vitellia realises that Sesto hasn't betrayed her. She understands the extent of his love and is torn between fear and remorse. As she dithers, Servilia sings to her in gentle reproach. In 'S' altro che lagrime' (If nothing but tears) she reminds Vitellia that weeping will achieve nothing; this pity the empress-to-be shows might as well be cruelty.

Left alone, Vitellia faces her moment of truth. The volatile princess whose self-absorbed tunnel-vision has caused so much unhappiness now sees what she has done to Sesto. In a long and dramatic accompanied recitative she realises she will always be haunted by Sesto and constantly living in fear, afraid that even the wind and the stones will give her away.

The great aria 'Non più di fiori' (Flowers no more) is a moment of calm inner vision in which she bids a long farewell to her greatness. Now that Vitellia is free of hysteria, self-pity takes over. Mozart provided a basset-horn obbligato for his friend Stadler in an aria more decorative than searingly emotional. The aria ends with interplay between voice and instrument that might grace a comic opera. It seems somehow suitable that what should be the emotional and psychological high-point of the opera is an ornate display piece; and that what might have filled out Vitellia as a complex and many-faceted character is merely another piece of narcissistic self-indulgence. Even Elettra in *Idomeneo* is more interesting.

However, the music leads straight into the superbly pompous orchestral prelude to the last scene: the amphitheatre, with a glimpse of the arena where the conspirators are to suffer the extreme penalty. The Roman people join in magnificent chorus of thanksgiving for the Emperor's well-being. Religious devoutness blends with terrestrial splendour in a direct reference to the occasion celebrated by the opera itself: an imperial coronation. Vitellia throws herself at Tito's feet and confesses her role in the plot (the Emperor, in a moment of possibly unconscious humour, wonders how many more people there are plotting against him) and assumes the greatest share of guilt.

In a long accompanied recitative the Emperor acts true to form. He orders all the conspirators to be freed. Sesto launches the finale with the sorrowful assertion that he will never forgive himself. Tito declares that true repentance is worth more even than uncomplicated loyalty. As all praise Tito and ask the gods to protect him, the Emperor affirms that the good of Rome shall be his eternal care.

A puzzle

So ends the puzzling opera that is *La Clemenza di Tito*. Puzzling because it is a sedate game of statuesque ciphers into which Mozart has sporadically breathed the life of human emotions; puzzling because he is happier when treating a public drama as a private tragedy; and puzzling because some ravishing music doesn't always seem entirely appropriate to the characters or the action.

The opera is also tantalising for its hint of the greatness that Mozart could have brought to the work if he had not been ill, tired and desperately worried by money troubles. Three strands of inspiration can be discerned in the score: Mozart on auto-pilot (mercifully rare), going expertly through the motions and doing what was artistically and socially expected of the composer of a coronation celebration; Mozart almost ignoring the libretto and writing beautiful music, however tenuous its relationship to the theatrical situation; and Mozart matching music to words, situation and character as only he could.

We must be grateful for Sesto and Annio's friendship duet, the wistful farewell declaration of love for Annio and Servilia, the great display arias for Sesto and Vitellia, the prelude and chorus in the last scene and the unexpected surge of dramatic impetus that carries the Act 1 finale forward. Had he lived to revise the work, Mozart might have made Vitellia into a more coherent character instead of a walking ego with some fine music to sing. He might have introduced more psychological variety into the role of Tito himself.

The Emperor was polite if rather cool. This time there was little to keep Mozart in Prague, especially as there are accounts which describe his health deteriorating alarmingly. The composer kept himself constantly stoked up with medicines, which may explain another hint which has survived over the centuries of the manic-depressive side of his nature, the 'gay seriousness' that seems to have characterised him more and more.

Still, perhaps surprisingly, whatever the views of the Empress, the opera caught on with the public in loyal Mozartian Prague. On his return to Vienna, the exhausted Mozart was cheered by the news of audience enthusiasm for *Clemenza*, just as *Die Zauberflöte* achieved its triumphant opening. It must have looked as if the tide of his fortunes had turned at last.

Chapter 9

The End of the Quest
The Magic Flute (2)

The glimpses we get of Mozart preparing his solemn, funny, moralistic pantomime are reassuring. He was evidently happy with Schikaneder's company of actors and singers, which included the composer and musician Benedikt Schackt (as Tamino) and his sister-in-law Josefa Hofer (another of the Weber sisters) as the Queen of the Night. He was also relatively unfazed by the erratic nature of the libretto, which lurches from folksy doggerel via masonic symbolism to warm-hearted moralising, and seized the chance to write music of an amazing diversity of styles. The most populist audience he had ever dealt with responded with delight. The first performance at the Theater auf der Wieden on September 30 1791 announced a palpable hit. It was to be the greatest popular success of Mozart's life.

Characters:
Tamino, a prince *tenor*
The Queen of the Night *soprano*
Pamina, her daughter *soprano*
Sarastro
Papageno, a bird-catcher *baritone*
Papagena *soprano*
Monostatos, a Moor *tenor*
The Speaker of the Temple *bass-baritone*
Three Ladies, Three Boys, Two Priests, Two Armed Men

Pantomime or philosophy?

Fairy-tale or philosophy? Pantomime or profundity? *The Magic Flute* delights children with its enchanted bells, funny birdman and apparently straightforward battle between nice and nasty. Adults can see it as charting an individual progress to enlightenment, the search for fulfilment as a complete human being. Schickaneder and Mozart aimed at both reactions. The former, taking the role of the birdman Papageno himself, underlined the gags and spectacular stage effects; and both librettist and composer collaborated in bringing the mysteries of Freemasonry, with its emphasis on liberty of thought and the fellowship of enlightenment, to the public stage.

Today it works best presented as an enchanting and enchanted fable: play it as a child's tale and the deeper messages emerge with moving clarity. The sources of the story include a *singspiel* called *Oberon* (for magic instruments) and a recently translated novel of ancient Egypt, *Sethos*, while the eminent mineralogist Ignaz von Born had anticipated the sentiments of Sarastro in an essay on the mysteries of the Freemasons. Elements can be found in other fairy-story operas and *singspiels*: half-human creatures, enchanted flutes, spirits and genies were heralding aspects of the Romantic age.

Act 1

The start of the overture seems misleadingly portentous. It brings trombones back to the opera-house pit after their successful use in *Don Giovanni*. The opening deploys three solemn chords, a foretaste of the ritualistic trials the hero and heroine will undergo in their quest for wisdom, and then plunges into a bustling fugue.

A rocky landscape. Tamino runs on with a bow but no arrows, pursued by a serpent (the original directions specify sumptuous Japanese costume for Tamino – one wonders how much did eighteenth-century Europe know of Japan? – and a temple in the background). Tamino cries for help and faints.

Three Ladies appear and kill the serpent, after which they admire the unconscious youth and promptly start squabbling over who shall keep watch over him and who shall go to tell their mistress, the Queen of the Night. Their music reflects changing emotions – martial for the despatch of the serpent, coyly amorous speculation, schoolgirl one-upmanship – before they reluctantly realise that, since they will never agree, they had better all go to the Queen together.

Tamino comes to, still dazed, sees the dead serpent and, hearing pan-pipes, nervously withdraws to watch the new arrival (Tamino has so far shown an endearing lack of machismo for a romantic hero). This is Papageno, half man, half bird, who lives by catching feathered creatures for the Queen of the Night. His song of introduction ('Der

Costume design for the bird-man Papageno in *The Magic Flute*.

The original cast for *The Magic Flute*, with Schikaneder as Papageno.

Vogelfänger bin ich ja'), one of the best known Mozart wrote, has a jolly, Haydnesque simplicity. In it Papageno cheerfully fantasises about catching girls as well as birds, especially that special girl who has eluded him so far.

In spoken dialogue Papageno bluffly presents himself as a man like any other, unimpressed by Tamino's revelation that he's a prince. Papageno also claims to have killed the serpent, at which the Ladies reappear and punish him for lying. After giving him water and stone instead of wine and cake, they padlock his mouth.

They present Tamino with a portrait of the Queen of the

Night's daughter, Pamina, and leave him to fall in love with her, as expressed in the rapt, wondering aria, 'Dies Bildnis' (This portrait is so beautiful). He is evidently overheard, for the three Ladies pop up again to inform him that the Queen has entrusted him with the task of finding Pamina, who has been abducted by a fiend.

Thunder announces the arrival of the Queen herself as the mountains part to reveal her on a starry throne. She reassures the young man in a grieving recitative ('O zittre nicht' – Tremble not) and launches into a sorrowful aria about her daughter's kidnapping. Only the hysterical coloratura climax (the aria is harder to sing than the flashier and more famous vengeance aria later on) hints that there is something sinister about this bereaved mother. She vanishes to the sound of thunder.

The inarticulately mouthing Papageno begins the quintet that ends the scene. The three Ladies remove the padlock and sing a brief moral about lies and slander. Tamino is given a golden flute that brings joy to all hearers. The reluctant Papageno is instructed to accompany the prince on his quest. To soften the blow, he receives a chime of bells. The Ladies add that three beautiful and wise young boys will guide the pair on their journey to the castle of Sarastro, the villain who holds Pamina captive. The men bid farewell to the Ladies and begin their search.

In Sarastro's castle

So far most of the music has been appropriate to a fairy-story, in a folksy, yarn-spinning vein, with moments of finger-wagging gravity when lessons are to be remembered. The second scene introduces us to a mood of exotic adventure leading to solemn rites. In Sarastro's castle (in a splendid room in the Egyptian style, according to the libretto) Pamina has been caught trying to escape and chains have been ordered by Monostatos, the rascally overseer.

Monostatos is that eighteenth-century fancy, a blackamoor, and therefore something of an embarrassment to modern producers. Sometimes references to his colour are deleted, sometimes he is simply played as white (occasionally, as in a London production, opposite a black Tamino). Portrayed as a stylised period convention, almost a decorative motif like the Marschallin's black page in *Der Rosenkavalier,* the concept can be inoffensive. It all depends on current sensibilities and whatever political correctness holds sway.

Certainly Papageno, who enters while Monostatos is

gloating over the fainting Pamina, is terrified by him; but then the Moor is appalled by the sight of the birdman. Each turns tail and runs; but Papageno ventures back with the politically just acceptable observation that there are black birds in the world so why not black people?

He informs Pamina that a gallant rescuer is at hand and adds that he (Papageno) could pull his feathers out in frustration for the lack of a woman in his life. Pamina comforts him in the duet 'Bei Männern' (Men who feel love). The music's grave sweetness lies somewhere between hymn and folksong as princess and clown agree that there is nothing nobler than the relationship of man and woman, and that love between them can attain the divine.

To the Temple of Wisdom

The words plant the idea of spiritual fulfilment in our mind, and it comes as no surprise that the scene changes to a grove in front of three temples. The Temple of Wisdom is flanked by those of Reason and Nature. Tamino is led in by the three Boys. Today they are usually sung by real choirboys with unbroken voices – with variable results: lucky Vienna has the Vienna Boys' Choir to call on, but some of us still shudder at the memory of the puny off-key yowling at Covent Garden some years ago. The alternative is to use young female singers, and a surprising number of great artists have cut their operatic teeth on the child-like serenity of this music. Production-wise, the Boys offer a producer a wide scope of picturesque possibilities, from flowered gondolas to balloons, when they arrive from the heavens.

With youthful solemnity the Boys advise Tamino to be steadfast. If he acts like a man he shall conquer like a man. They leave him to approach the Temple of Reason, after a heroic recitative that elevates the mood from fairy-tale to mystic ritual. Voices from within urge him back. He is similarly rejected at the Temple of Nature. But from the central temple the Speaker emerges. He interrogates the prince and hints that Tamino may have been misinformed about Sarastro. He will find out only by reaching the sanctuary and the inner brotherhood.

He withdraws, and the bewildered Tamino's harrowing cry of 'O ew'ge Nacht' (Eternal night) indicates how serious the mood has become. Yet the unseen voices give him some hope: they tell him Pamina is still alive, and he joyfully plays the magic flute. All sorts of animals shyly approach to listen (a gift of a scene to a producer). Papageno's panpipes answer him off-stage. He hastens away, just missing the birdman and the princess as they hurry on. Trying to contact Tamino by pipe-call, they are surprised by the odious Monostatos. He calls slaves with bonds and chains, but Papageno decides to try out the magic bells; they immediately cast a spell on the Moor and the slaves, who find themselves singing and dancing, and prance off-stage in a state of euphoria.

Pamina and Papageno draw a moral from true harmony, and how the harmony of friendship, no less than that of music, can generate real happiness. The music trips along with a blend of almost child-like gravity and sweetness but suddenly a march is heard, drums and trumpets prominent. Both are frightened at the approach of Sarastro, but react in different ways. The terrified Papageno longingly thinks of a hole he could hide in like a mouse. Pamina is determined to tell the truth, even if it means being punished.

The chorus heralds Sarastro and it soon becomes apparent that he's no ogre. His music is mellow and dignified; but he refuses to return Pamina to her mother. Pamina's heart should be guided by a man, he adds, whereas her mother is a proud woman.

Tamino is led in by Monostatos. As in all fairy-tales, the young couple fall rapturously in love at first sight. They promptly embrace, to the outrage of the Moor; but he is ordered to be flogged for his misdeeds. Sarastro's domain begins to look safe and fair. As Monostatos is dragged away, Sarastro announces that the young couple must be purified, and the chorus sings of the virtue and justice that enables mankind to approach the divine. To these lofty preparations for initiation the curtain falls.

Act 2

The scene is a forest of gold and silver palms, with pyramids. Sarastro and the priests enter to the sound of a march. In spoken dialogue Sarastro proposes Tamino as a member of the brotherhood. The others assent and horns sound three times – the masons' significant number – before Sarastro expounds on how Tamino's membership will end prejudice and ignorance (the Freemasons are obviously speaking here).

The gods have ordained Pamina for him, which is why he has removed her from her deceitful mother – who stands for superstition and trickery (perhaps a reference to the reactionary reign of the late Empress Maria Theresa). The three chords are repeated twice more in this scene as Sarastro reassures his colleagues on the worthiness of the young prince ('more than that, he is a human!'). Sarastro's 'O Isis und Osiris' asks the gods to give the young pair wisdom and strength. The tone of the aria is both noble and warm-hearted, in what one might call Mozart's fairy-tale or mythological mode: kindly, straightforward and humane.

Night. A ruined landscape. Tamino and Papageno are led in by priests who remove their blindfolds (sacks in the original libretto) and leave them. Tamino urges his gibbering companion to be a man. The Speaker and a priest enter with torches. In response to their questions, Tamino declares himself ready to submit to ordeals in search of friendship, wisdom, love – and Pamina. Papageno on the other hand emphatically declines the ordeals, nor is he really after wisdom, thank you very much. He's happy eating, drinking and sleeping; though a wife would be nice too. When he's informed that a wife is waiting for him, coincidentally named Papagena, he's torn between fear and curiosity. The two priests impose an oath of silence on the pair, and in a duet warn the two adventurers of the wiles of women – not the last time that misogynist sentiments are uttered in the opera.

The relationship between Tamino and Papageno emerges clearly now: the serious and valiant hero, his mind set on higher things, and his earthier side-kick, a Sancho Panza figure who would settle for a quiet life and longs to be out of this mysterious darkness with its tests and ordeals.

His qualms are not soothed by the sudden appearance of the Three Ladies urging the men to escape and foretelling death for them both. Tamino scrupulously observes his vow not to speak to women. In a quintet he refuses to heed their prophecies of doom, while Papageno is just held back from talking to them. The Three Ladies are baffled. Ominous chords and cries of outrage from the priests within speed them on their way. The Speaker enters and, commending Tamino's steadfastness, leads him blindfolded to the next adventure. The prince rallies the cowering Papageno in lighter vein; and the birdman follows, grumbling that all this wandering about just to get his Papagena is enough to put him off love forever.

The Queen of the Night

The scene switches to a garden where Pamina is asleep in a bower. Monostatos steals in and admires her beauty. In a little aria ('Alles fühlt der Lieberfreuden' – Everyone enjoys love), Mozart shows his sympathy, as he nearly always does even with the least likeable characters. Monostatos complains

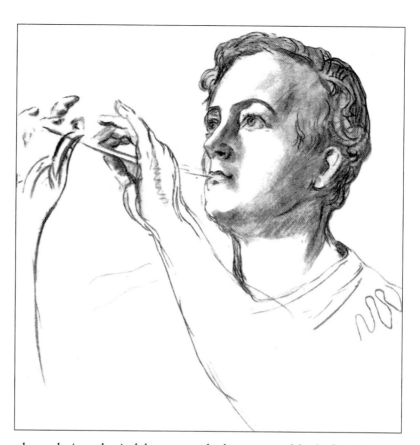

Thorkild Norval as Tamino at pre-war Glyndebourne.

about being denied love merely because a black face is considered ugly (and adds the now highly incorrect sentiment that 'weiss ist schön' – white is beautiful). He is creeping up to Pamina to steal a kiss when the Queen of the Night appears to a clap of thunder. The slave hides and proceeds to eavesdrop on the conversation between mother and long-lost daughter. The Queen produces a dagger and urges Pamina to kill Sarastro; only thus can the Queen regain the power that her late husband, Pamina's father, handed over to him. She launches into the famous vengeance aria, 'Die Hölle Rache' (Hellish revenge) with its dazzling vocal pyrotechnics that hit high F.

This aria, with the less famous first act outburst, poses problems as regards casting the role. Sopranos with the agility and range to sing the notes accurately tend to be lightweight, bright in tone, and not always capable of expressing demonic rage – one of the most famous current exponents of the part at Covent Garden in recent seasons merely sounded like a demented canary (even Joan Sutherland, who has the richness of tone and the ideal agility, came a critical cropper in the role at Covent Garden). Singers capable of packing a dramatic punch tend to lack the flexibility and the high notes. There have been exceptions: the Hungarian Maria Nemeth, a great Turandot and Aida, hurled out the Queen's imprecations in pre-war Germany, while Pauline Tinsley, a cutting-voiced Verdi heroic soprano, tackled the role in Britain in the 1960s.

The Queen vanishes, leaving her bewildered daughter clutching the dagger. Monostatos leaps forward and attempts to blackmail Pamina. When she continues to repulse him, he raises the knife to stab her, but is stopped by Sarastro's entrance. The blackamoor scurries off, determined to throw his lot in with the Queen, while Sarastro calms Pamina with the assurance that he knows the whole story. In a serenely noble aria ('In diesen heil'gen Hallen' – Within these holy walls) he consolingly sings of forgiveness, not revenge, and the path back to righteousness via love and friendship.

The novitiates

The next scene opens with the two blindfolded novitiates being led in by priests who warn them again to observe silence, and leave them to await the signal for their next step, the sound of trombones. As usual, Papageno can't keep quiet for long. He complains of the lack of even a drop of water, at which an ugly crone appears with a beakerful. Her affectionate manner and assertion that she's only eighteen prompt the birdman to ask her jokingly if she has a sweetheart. She replies that it's Papageno – himself – and hobbles away, leaving him dismayed.

The Three Boys enter in 'a flying machine decked with roses', returning the flute and magic bells to the intrepid pair. Unlike the Ladies, they are on Sarastro's side. They encourage our heroes, incidentally producing a table laden with food and wine. In the subsequent dialogue, Papageno tucks in with a will but Tamino holds himself aloof, preferring to make magic music on the flute.

The sound of it attracts Pamina. Her joy at finding Tamino is shattered by his silence: even Papageno gesticulates at her, his mouth full, to go away. The broken-hearted girl, believing herself abandoned, gives vent to her feelings in a hauntingly lovely aria of desolate grief, 'Ach ich fühl's' (I feel it has vanished) in which she laments the demise of love and longs for the peace of death; one of those heart-touching moments where Mozart transcends the particular dramatic situation and reaches a higher, more universal, level.

Tamino must be suffering a gut-wrenching temptation to respond but he holds fast even when the weeping girl runs from the stage. Only Papageno prattles cheerfully as he guzzles. He ignores the three trombone chords that summon the adventurers to the next stage of their quest. Only on the third chord does Tamino manage to drag his protesting sidekick off.

In the vault of the pyramid the priests sing a chorus to Isis and Osiris in music serene, calm and confident. Tamino and Pamina are led in separately and Sarastro orders the girl to bid her beloved a final farewell. In a trio Sarastro reassures the loving Pamina and her stalwart prince that they will meet again with joy; but now duty calls.

In a scene-change we find Papageno, by now lost and alone, admitting to the Speaker that at the moment his greatest desire in life is a glass of wine. The priest magically obliges and leaves the birdman to meditate on the dream of a little girl-friend or wife ('Ein Mädchen oder Weibchen'): a gentle dove to keep him company, a female mouth to kiss, and he'd be as happy as any prince.

The old crone hobbles in as if on cue and declares their match already made – a bit too much of a good thing for Papageno until she explains that if he refuses her she'll be imprisoned here forever, alone, living on bread and water. Papageno promptly swears eternal faithfulness to her, at which the old hag suddenly changes into a Papagena, a sweet little female version of the birdman. The Speaker prevents their embrace as Papageno is not yet worthy of her. When Papageno flamboyantly (and rather unwisely, given the present unpredictable circumstances) declares that the earth can swallow him, it does so.

In a garden the Three Boys herald the dawn of both the sun and enlightenment in radiantly pure tones ('Bald prängt'). They decide to console the unhappy Pamina, who enters, clasping her mother's dagger, beside herself with sorrow and intent on suicide. The boys stop her, assure her that Tamino loves her, and lead her to the next stage of the adventure.

Pamina and Tamino

A spectacular transformation scene gives us two mountains. Down one cascades a torrential waterfall while the other belches fire. Two armed men escort Tamino in. In a religious-sounding chorale they sing of how purification awaits the traveller if only he can conquer his fear. Pamina runs in and the lovers are at last allowed to speak to each other. At their embrace the music becomes warmer and more expansive. Pamina takes his hand, not simply a companion but a guide. She bids Tamino play the flute – made by her father from a thousand-year-old oak – that will protect them.

Pamina's emergence as a positive force in the ritual ordeals owes much to Mozart. The Masons themselves were traditionally sceptical about of women's abilities to participate in the pursuit of enlightenment, and the libretto of *The Magic Flute* is full of remarks that strike us as pretty sexist these days. But from now on, as most stage productions make clear, Pamina takes the lead, proving a worthy partner for Tamino, and an equal.

The two wander through the fire and water; the music is stately rather than menacing, ritualistic rather than dramatic. This is no supernatural threat like Neptune's anger in *Idomeneo*, but a grave and dignified rite of passage, permeated by the feeling of confident determination shown by the young couple.

The door to the inner temple opens, revealing dazzling splendour (or, in sober modern productions, the plain brightness of self-knowledge). The chorus hails the noble pair's triumph and the two are invited into the temple.

Meanwhile, what of the earthier progress by the more mundane specimens of humanity? Back in the garden Papageno is looking for his Papagena, calling and playing his panpipes to summon her. In vain. In his own way, and on his own level, Papageno too now knows the dark night of the soul. How could such joy be promised, such happiness glimpsed, only to be snatched away again? The scene is a gift to a good singing actor, a mixture of comedy and pathos; and the latter is important, for though Papageno's aspirations are not very high, he too has searched his soul, or what passes for it, and known longing and grief.

At the moment he's at the end of his tether – a hempen tether, almost literally, since he unties the rope from round his waist and throws it over the branch of a tree preparatory to suicide. Being Papageno, of course, he plays for time, hoping someone or something will turn up to stop him. He decides to count up to ten, intermittently playing on his pipes.

Just as he despairingly makes for the rope the Three Boys fly in to remind him of his magic bells. While he chimes hopefully they bring in Papagena. Their enchanting little duet, which usually brings the house down, opening with the incredulous, bird-like cries of 'Pa-Pa-Pa', defines their happily undemanding life as they look forward to domestic bliss with lots of little Papageni. Like Shakespeare, Mozart can illuminate the common man and the desires of little people while portraying great issues and the profound emotions of the

Mozart's death-bed. A very romanticised nineteenth-century image of the composer dictating the *Requiem* to the last, flanked by the symbolically empty song-bird cage (left) and the clock (right).

elevated . . . . Without Papageno and Papagena, the enlightened world of Tamino and Pamina would be incomplete. They may settle down in contented obscurity like the Pooters of the operatic world, but Mozart reminds us that even the diary of a nobody is written by a very alive somebody.

Evil overthrown

It only remains, as in the best fairy-stories, for evil to be seen to be defeated. The Queen of the Night, Monostatos and the Three Ladies sneak on ('Nur stille, stille, stille, stille!') in an attempt to break into the temple: in return for his treachery the Moor has been promised Pamina's hand. Their plans to massacre the pious come to nothing as the conspirators are put to flight by thunder and lightning. The final tableau, illuminated by the great symbol of the sun, shows Pamina and Tamino united; while Sarastro and the chorus praise the light that dispels darkness and the virtue that decks beauty and

wisdom with an eternal crown.

Ordinary townspeople – not lords and ladies, still less emperors and kings – had given Mozart his greatest success. Ill and exhausted, he still had time to realise it, even though he suspected he would have little time to relish it fully. 'I have come to the end before having enjoyed my talent,' he noted. 'Life was so lovely, my career opened under such happy auspices, but one cannot change one's destiny.' He loved teasing his friends in the company, exemplified by the occasion when he took over the offstage glockenspiel to which Papageno mimes his magic chimes. Mozart played an arpeggio when Papageno (Schikaneder) was pausing. The actor spotted Mozart in the wings and they improvised some amusing business with the unpredictable chimes, to the audience's delight.

Mozart even took Salieri to a performance. We can only imagine his satisfaction as the Italian appeared to enjoy the

The last portrait of Mozart, aged thirty-three, made by Dora Stock when he visited Leipzig in 1789.

whole thing – 'there was not a single number that did not call forth from him a "bravo" or a "bello".' Yet it was at this time that, walking in the Prater with Constanze, Mozart began to cry and told her that he suspected he had been poisoned. Other friends and acquaintances noticed his gloom and preoccupation with death. Miraculously he wrote the effortlessly beautiful concerto for his clarinettist friend Stadler before turning his attention fully to the Requiem.

Illness and death

The devoted Süssmayer helped his master in the agonising business of composing from a sickbed. Mozart's hands and feet became swollen and partly paralysed, and he suffered fits of vomiting. In the evenings when *The Magic Flute* was playing he would work out which point of the story the performance had reached at any time, but soon it became a race against time to finish the Requiem. There was a rehearsal round his bed on December 4; he broke down and wept while singing in the Lacrimosa. The theatre doctor was called but could do nothing. At five to one on the morning of December 5 1791 the small figure with distended stomach suffered a final convulsion and spewed out an arc of liquid.

Such was the passing of Mozart, who had given such beauty to the world. At the time it was believed he had died of rheumatic fever; subsequent opinions have tended to progressive kidney failure. The swollen body provoked rumours of poison; and in his dotage Salieri rambled insanely about killing Mozart, but there's no evidence for the myth of the older man murdering his younger rival (there was only six years difference in their ages, despite the usual portrayal of them as belonging to different generations).

The so-called 'pauper's grave' legend seems now to have been prompted by a normal, inexpensive funeral, often opted for by the less pretentious and more enlightened. There was a short memorial service in St Stephen's Cathedral at which fellow-masons and others, including Salieri, were present. The Emperor provided a pension, the King of Prussia bought manuscripts, there were benefit concerts, including a Mozart piano concerto played by the young Beethoven.

Constanze has traditionally had a bad press, perhaps stemming from her father-in-law's disapproval, but as a widow she worked tirelessly on behalf of her husband's music. One can only wonder what Amadé would have thought at her entrusting the musical education of his sons to Salieri. She married again and outlived her first husband by fifty years. They had two surviving sons. Franz Xaver became a composer; Karl Thomas became an imperial civil servant and died in Italy, part of the bureaucracy of Austrian occupation against which the Risorgimento would revolt. His estates in Italy had been bought with the royalties from a French revival of *Figaro*; but then it's been enriching us all for over two hundred years.

Tito was – strangely, in view of its disappearance for over a hundred years until revivals in the 1940s – one of the most popular Mozart operas abroad immediately after his death. The nineteenth century loved *Don Giovanni,* with *Figaro* coming a close second. *Così fan tutte*, with its awkward ambiguities and apparently blandly-charted heartbreak also vanished in nineteenth century, though the late twentieth has made it into a box office standby.

Mozart has become the object of cults, musicological

research, psycho-analysis; he has featured in plays by writers as diverse as Pushkin and Peter Shaffer; the recording industry has opened new horizons by unearthing the unfinished or the unstageworthy among his operas. We can choose between warm Italianate Mozart, plushly nineteenth century, or exhilaratingly abrasive 'authentic' period sound. However you take your Mozart – dry, neat or with all the trimmings – the genius shines through.

Chapter 10

Remembrance and Reassessment:
The man and his music

'He is one of the most charming creatures that you could wish to see: everything he does and says is full of life and soul . . . by his gaiety he even removes the fear that one may have that so ripe a fruit might fall before its full maturity. If these children live . . . soon the sovereigns will quarrel over possessing them.'

So wrote the Baron Grimm of the two Mozart children, brother and sister, during their tours as prodigies. They lived; but the sovereigns found adult musicians less appealing than child wonders. Wolfgang's sister Nannerl married a titled nobleman and lived on to a ripe old age, but it is the character of her short-lived brother that has passed into the realm of conjecture and legend. He was the enchanting boy who never quite grew up.

The respectable nineteenth century enjoyed secretly disapproving of what it considered must have been his fecklessness. For the less respectable, the Romantics for instance, he was the archetypal artist, misunderstood and unappreciated in his lifetime but subject to a divine compulsion. All have agreed that his fame fizzled out and his fortune was nonexistent; the myth of the pauper's burial – actually a 'third-class' funeral like the majority of the time – has helped.

In fact Mozart earned a respectable amount but loved fine clothes, and his fondness for billiards may have led to gambling, one of the passions of the time. Both his poverty and his apparent fecklessness have been exaggerated – the latter by his widow and sister, who liked to portray the family as a steadying influence. It's not too flippant to suppose that Mozart's shortness – one English visitor described him as about five foot four inches in height – might, as with many small people, have intensified his assertiveness, adding a pugnacity to his resentfulness at being treated like a servant or not given his professional due. As a

Mozart's funeral: subsequently much sentimentalised, this appears to have been the functional, no-frills funeral in favour with the intelligentsia of the time.

child he wanted to be loved – this is not retrospective psycho-analysis: we know that he cried if the grownups he was fond of pretended not to love him.

Perpetually in motion

The play and film of *Amadeus* have reminded us of the young man's smutty jokes and his lavatorial humour. He could certainly be ebullient. At fifteen, staying in Venice, he described some horseplay with the daughters of the house where he lodged: 'To become a true Venetian you have to encounter the "*attacca*" – you must let yourself be bumped on the ground and then smacked behind. They tried to do it to me, all seven wenches together, but the whole seven didn't succeed in throwing me down.' A few months later he had the energy to learn deaf and dumb language, 'and I can do these signs to perfection', to converse with the deaf and dumb son of his Milanese

landlord. In an obituary, which incidentally provides his first biography with facts gleaned from his sister, he was described as 'perpetually in motion . . . either playing with his hands or beating the ground with his foot'. Those brilliant pianist's hands were clumsy at everyday tasks: his wife even carved for him at table.

In most respects, we are informed, Mozart 'remained a child. He never knew properly how to conduct himself.' This allegedly spilled over into his practical affairs, particularly his management of money. 'The gratification of the moment was always uppermost with him,' we are primly reminded. 'His mind was so obsessed with a crowd of ideas, which rendered him incapable of all serious reflection, that during his whole life he stood in need of a guardian of his temporal affairs.' One can hear the disapproving note of bourgeois respectability, thrift and foresight echoing down the years.

Even the fondly reminiscent Johann Andreas Schachtner, the court musician who had teased the little boy with his trumpet, opines rather starchily that 'his inclinations were easily swayed: I believe that had he lacked the advantage of the good education which he received, he might have become a profligate scoundrel – he was so ready to yield to every attraction which offered.' There were even rumours of sexual infidelity, especially when enjoying the company of Schikaneder's troupe during the composition of *The Magic Flute*. At any rate, Mozart paid dearly for the pace at which he conducted both work and pleasure. His last months were riddled with melancholy and, yes, though the crime itself is almost certainly a myth, he was haunted by the idea of being poisoned.

Mozartmania

Yet the image of the neglected and discounted little man whose virtues were realised only in the next century scarcely squares with a slightly resentful observation published in the German provinces in 1794, a mere three years after his death, that music by Mozart was all people wanted to hear. The article even speaks of 'Mozartmania'. Unlike many great artists, Mozart was not immediately forgotten at his death to be rediscovered by subsequent generations: he never quite went away, even though his music, like the personality of the man himself, was subject to a wide range of interpretation.

Apart from the changes in fashion and style brought about by time, there are temperamental differences between races that can contribute to the fluctuating fortunes of a great artist's reputation. Stendhal made a celebrated comment that Mozart's music was 'not calculated for the climate of Italy'. Certainly any opera-goer who has sat through a restive Italian audience's impatience for the big, walloping tunes that never come and the chattering recitative that does, will bear that out. Maria Callas would lavish artistry on Puccini and Giordano, but sang only one Mozart role on stage (Constanze in an Italian *The Seraglio* at La Scala) and professed to find him 'boring'. There's a certain irony in this, given that Mozart's greatest operatic creations are born of the Italian opera conventions of his day: he was far more of an Italian melodist than a German classicist. Today most singers both revere and fear the clarity and accuracy Mozart's music needs above all. You can't fudge it, as you can (as even reputable musicians will admit) Puccini or even Verdi. Mozart's vocal line mercilessly exposes any weakness, and his operas are seen as the touchstone of a singer's technique.

Georg Nikolaus Nissen: this Danish diplomat married Mozart's widow in 1809, and compiled material for a documentary life of Mozart, left incomplete at Nissen's death in 1826. His widow published the biography in 1828.

Within a year of his death post-revolutionary France had interpreted *The Magic Flute* in such a way as to reassure the modern opera-goer that 'concept' productions are nothing new. The Queen of the Night represented the *ancien régime*; Tamino was The People, Pamina 'Freedom as the Daughter of Despotism'; Sarastro embodied the 'Wisdom of a Better Legislation'; and the Priests were the National Assembly (one can only wonder at the reception a modern production featuring our parliamentary legislators would have in these cynical days).

The more conventional masonic version of the opera tended to identify the Queen and Tamino as the Empress Maria Theresa and her son, Joseph II, while Pamina symbolised the Austrian people and Sarastro the Grand Master Ignaz von Born. The sober nineteenth century rather frowned on the clowning of Papageno and Papagena. In our own time the most successful productions have taken the work at face value: a moral fairy-tale, both funny and touching; and artists as great and various as Chagall, Kokoschka and Hockney have captured its spirit in their designs, while the Bergman film has succeeded in gaining a wider audience than opera usually achieves.

Not all Mozart's operas needed topical interpretations or

special pleading. *The Seraglio* virtually made his name in Central Europe as an operatic composer: the period 1783-1785 saw the work performed in Prague, Leipzig, Frankfurt, Bonn, Mannheim, Salzburg, Dresden, Munich and Kassel. Germany took to *Don Giovanni* – but in German. Already in the composer's lifetime a rather coarse version rechristened the Don as 'Hans von Schwankenreich' and Leporello as 'Fickfack'. The neo-classicism of the time guaranteed *Tito* a widespread success in the 1790s (it moved Goethe's mother to tears), but it disappeared in the nineteenth century and even its reappearance at the 1949 Salzburg Festival fell flat.

Così, as already noted, vanished, its beautiful ambiguities and sad, smiling acceptance of human frailty leaving both idealist Romantics and the correct middle classes uncomfortable. It has emerged in our own century as a box office favourite, its graceful mixture of tenderness and cynicism tailor-made for our disillusioned times. *Figaro* was the first opera to be performed at the Paris Opéra after the Revolution. The recitatives were replaced by dialogue from Beaumarchais' play, just as Molière's *Don Juan* would provide words for Mozart's *Don Giovanni*. These two works, along with the *Flute*, kept Mozart's operatic reputation alive in the century after his death.

Mozart in the twentieth century

The twentieth century has canonised Mozart – not always for the right reasons – and paid his operas the compliment of producing and re-producing them in styles that range from exquisitely swagged rococo (post-war Glyndebourne) to a reflection of inner-city drugs and violence (the American director Peter Sellars). The international summer festivals at Salzburg, Glyndebourne and to a lesser extent Aix have garnished Mozart with chic and snobbery as well as artistic dedication, while the bread and butter repertory of normal opera houses could never do without its *Flute* or *Figaro*. Little Amadé seems safe on his pedestal, as safe as any 'classic' can be in the whirligig of time and taste.

Yet it is still hard to put his operas in context. They acknowledge the spare, emotional tautness of Gluck but, apart perhaps from the classical dignity of *Idomeneo* and *Tito*, are nothing like the older composer's work. They drink in Italian sunshine with its limpid melody and chattering comedy, but could never be mistaken for the work of an Italian: the orchestral refinement and the sudden heart-touching turn of a phrase bespeak a more melancholy and introspective genius. Draw a line of descent tracing the evolution of opera and Mozart will fit in uneasily. Beethoven's *Fidelio* and the operas of Weber (the cousin of Mozart's wife) spring from the same *genus* as *The Magic Flute* but lack that work's mastery of many musical forms, from farce to religious hymn. Sometimes you hear the echo of Mozart in the patter of Rossini comedy; sometimes an arch-Romantic like Berlioz will remind you, with a wheedling phrase or crystalline texture, that he loved Mozart too. But Mozart had no single direct ancestor; and he has been eclipsed by none of his descendants.

A Mozart Opera Chronology

1756: Wolfgang Amadeus Mozart born in Salzburg

1757: Leopold Mozart becomes Court composer at Salzburg

1761: Mozart's first composition

1762: Mozart family tour to Munich

1763: Mozart family tour to Paris

1764: Publication of Mozart's first printed works

1768: First performance of *Bastien und Bastienne*

1769: First performance of *La finta semplice*

1770: First performance of *Mitridate, re di Ponto*

1772: First performance of *Il sogno di Scipione* and *Lucio Silla*

1775: First performance of *La finta giardiniera* and *Il re pastore*

1778: Composed *Semiramis* (now lost)

1781: First performance of *Idomeneo*

1782: First performance of *The Abduction from the Seraglio*

1783: Worked on *L'oca del Cairo* and *Lo sposo deluso*

1786: First performance of *Der Schauspieldirektor* and *The Marriage of Figaro*

1787: First performance of *Don Giovanni*

1790: First performance of *Così fan Tutte*

1791: First performance of *La Clemenza di Tito* and *The Magic Flute*; death of Mozart

Further Reading

Anderson, Emily (ed. and transl.): *The Letters of Mozart and his Family*, 3rd edn. revised by Stanley Sadie and Fiona Smart, London 1985

Brophy, Brigid: *Mozart the Dramatist*, London 1988

Dent, Edward J.: *Mozart's Operas*, London 1962

Deutsch, Otto Erich: *Mozart: A Documentary Biography*

—*Mozart and his World in Contemporary Pictures*, Kassel 1961

Landon, H. C. Robbins and Donald Mitchell: *The Mozart Companion*, Faber, London 1965

Mann, William: *The Operas of Mozart*, London 1977

Osborne, Charles: *The Complete Operas of Mozart: A Critical Guide*, London 1978

Sadie, Stanley: *Mozart*, London 1965

For individual operas the Opera Guides published by John Calder in association with the English National Opera and Royal Opera Covent Garden are highly recommended.

Index